I0156531

STOP
BEING INVISIBLE

Start Building a Human Brand of Greater Influence

DION MCINTOSH

Stop Being Invisible: Start building a human brand of greater influence.

Copyright © 2020 by Dion McIntosh.

All rights reserved under International and Pan-American Copyright Conventions. By payment of the required fees, you have been granted the nonexclusive, nontransferable right to access and read the text of this book. No part of this text may be reproduced, transmitted, downloaded, decompiled, reverse-engineered, or stored in or introduced into any information storage or retrieval system, in any form or by any means, whether electronic or mechanical, now known or hereafter invented without the express written permission of Bad People Books & Tapes.

First Edition

Cover design by Alex Santo
Author photograph courtesy of Dion McIntosh
Book Layout & eBook Conversion by manuscript2ebook.com

Library of Congress Cataloging-in-Publication Data
Names: McIntosh, Dion, author.
Title: Stop Being Invisible: Start building a human brand of greater influence. / Dion McIntosh
Description: First Edition. | Los Angeles : BadPeople, 2020.

Identifiers:

Subjects: LCSH: Entrepreneurship. | Success in business. | Influence (Psychology) | BISAC: BUSINESS & ECONOMICS / Entrepreneurship. | BUSINESS & ECONOMICS / E-Commerce / Internet Marketing. | SELF-HELP / Motivational & Inspirational.

Classification:

LC record available at

Digital Edition August 2020 ISBN: 978-7355830-1-3

Version 01012020

Print ISBN: 978-1-7355830-0-6

Hello, you beautiful human being! Did you know that you already have a brand? It is a reflection of you; and you are a reflection of it. This is an invaluable asset to your business prospects. The question is: Will you manage your brand—or will your brand manage you?

By simply being the author of your own story, you are taking charge and consciously, thoughtfully building your brand. This can mean all the difference between being seen and becoming known in the marketplace—or remaining invisible.

Besides the obvious personal benefits of shaping a well-known, influential human brand, you and your story can impact this world in ways you may not have considered. Your story is as unique as your DNA. If you don't tell it, the world is forever robbed of the unique contribution only you could have given to humanity. Besides elevating your business image, you brand story might help you:

- Disrupt and evolve your industry by sharing your unique methods

- Encourage someone to keep going who is close to quitting on their dream

- Inspire an artist to create art that touches the hearts of millions

- Be a hero to the disenfranchised or marginalized

- Give hope to a young person who needs to know they're not alone

- Save at least one person from suicide

- Be the voice of reason for someone who couldn't hear it from any other messenger

I'm deeply honored for the chance to help you tell your story. Thank you for picking up my book.

With humility and gratitude,

Dion McIntosh

WHO SHOULD READ THIS BOOK?

You should, if:

- You are currently building a business or project you're passionate about

- You want to increase your personal profile and influence in your industry

- You care about making a positive impact on the planet and/or its inhabitants

Stop Being Invisible will show you the basic building blocks of how to more clearly communicate who you really are, what you do, why you do it, and who you do it for—in a way that connects with the right humans.

These insights are based on my years of branding people and building businesses. This book is designed to work in tandem with the accompanying workbook to help you actually *do the work*, rather than just read the theory.

Note: If you jacked this book from a friend and want your own workbook you can download the PDF for free at www. DionMcIntosh.com/InvisibleWorkbook.

DEDICATION

*D*on't skip this section! I have found that listening to someone else express their gratitude and love for others can make me feel good and inspire me to do the same in my life. Please read this section, as it might remind you of someone you need to acknowledge in your world.

There are some humans I need to acknowledge for helping make this book a reality: my tribe. Let's start with my brothers in arms, Stefan Fincias and Alex Atescatenco. A mentor of mine, Brian Kaufman, (rest in peace) once told me that the best people in your life are the ones you can count on to be consistently reliable and honest with you over a long period of time. People you can be yourself with, laugh with, cry with, and enjoy life with—even when shit goes sideways. You two have proven to be those dudes for me, even when I fuck up. I've got mad love for you both and endeavor to be that dude for you gentlemen in return.

My daughters, Seven and Halo, and my son, Chosen: you incredible, enlightened beings have taught me how to love more deeply than I thought was possible. Without you three, I probably would have quit a long time ago. I'm proud of each of you. I'm so lucky to be your dad.

I'd like to thank my most important co-founder in life, my goddess, my wife, my best friend: Amy "Frankie Jordan" McIntosh. You have stood by me through more than most people could ever endure. You have helped me find my edge, and always push me to lean just beyond where I thought I couldn't push any further. None of this works without you. You call me on my bullshit, even when I don't see it right away. Your intuition has saved my ass countless times. You're a warrior queen. I'm still in awe of your strength and "take no shit " attitude. I wish I could be like you in this way. I'm actually a little afraid of you. I'm honored to be your husband.

Last, but certainly not least, my mom: Helen McIntosh. You gave me a lovely life. I learned so much by watching you never take no for an answer, and by overcoming crazy odds to accomplish your goals while setting me up for success. You gave me your wings so I could fly, and walked away from many of your own dreams to help me reach mine. I can never repay you for your sacrifice. I would not have been able to accomplish all that I have without your guidance throughout my life. I hope I made you proud, even though I never won that Grammy.

You all are my heart. My tribe. I'm your "ride or die" for life.

TABLE OF CONTENTS

INTRO

Let me start by establishing something very important: if you're building a business of any kind, a strong, human brand will always carry it further than obscure leadership will. I don't care if it's in entertainment, real estate, medical, design, marketing, coaching, legal, education, or any other industry, the companies run by at least one high-profile, influential industry expert will crush those run by lesser-known competitors. In fact, if *you* are a well-known, influential market expert in any business sector, you have a better shot at entering and dominating new markets than people who are not household names—people who may be more credible and talented than you are (I'll prove this one in a minute.)

We see adequate or mediocre social media influencers making millions, getting parts in movies, launching products, or cashing big endorsement checks while extremely talented, seasoned artists and entrepreneurs struggle to pay rent. Why? That superior brand. There are, of course, many reasons for success or failure beyond just being well-known. But being well-known most certainly carries huge advantages.

Besides just gaining you market success, though, building a strong, human brand can help you become synonymous with your industry. In other words: fame, meet fortune. This is why some folks dominate markets so hard that even the mention of the niche brings them to mind.

Consider the following two scenarios.

Do you know what Martin Eberhard and Marc Tarpenning created?

No?

Do electric cars bring anyone to mind? Doorbell! Who's there? It's Elon Musk with a joint in his mouth, standing on Mars!

Tesla Motors was actually the brainchild of Martin and Marc long before Elon came along. But most people only know Tesla as an Elon Musk company, and rightly so. He took it from the nerd lab to the stratosphere. Tesla and Elon are synonymous at this point. Elon and electric cars, in general, are synonymous.

How would you like your name to come to mind when folks think about your industry niche? Imagine the opportunities that would flow your way.

Now, let me ask: do you know Simona Cattaneo?

No?

Simona launched successful merch icons that include Gucci Bloom, Gucci Makeup, and the Tiffany & Co. fragrance line. Cattaneo has held senior positions at Burberry Beauty, Christian Dior Parfums, and L'Oréal. She is a serious C-suite player in the cosmetics game. She is presently also the CEO of Kylie Cosmetics. Her pedigree in the industry is top of the game.

But, whoooooooo cares?

Not the end user, that's for sure.

The consumers of Kylie Cosmetics only care about one person over there: Kylie. Kylie Jenner has no prior experience or industry credibility, no cosmetics or scientific formulation genius, and no unique talent. Her products have not revolutionized or disrupted the market in any way, other than sales. She's famous for being famous, and basically unremarkable compared to a powerhouse like Simona Cattaneo. This didn't stop Kylie from dominating the market, making hundreds of millions of dollars, and being considered a cosmetics mogul by some. If Simona tried launching a brand of her own, she couldn't come close to this type of scale so quickly.

How is this possible?

Simple. It all comes down to the power and influence of human branding. Over 150 million social media followers plus a huge reality show give Kylie the distribution network and public notoriety to push almost *any* product to the top of the charts. (Having a beast of a mom in her corner doesn't hurt either.)

Imagine for a moment that you had just a fraction of that pull in your industry—*and* you have actual talent or a unique I.P., along with some deep industry knowledge and experience. Don't you think you could accomplish a lot more in the world? Of course you could! 100 percent.

Now, I could fill a book with names and case studies to beat this ailing horse, but no one I've ever met likes beating horses. I realize that only a small percentage of humans will ever reach the level of a Kylie or Elon, for example, but even building a profile in a small niche can help you move the needle and accomplish greater things. There are countless influential folks you've never heard of in niches all around the world who took the opportunity to brand themselves and dominate their small slice of an industry. And there's no shortage of opportunity for you, if you want to do the same.

Before we dive in, I just want to say that there are plenty of success stories of faceless companies from a consumer-facing perspective that do just fine. But this book isn't for those who want to build a faceless company. It's for those who like the idea of having some spotlight, notoriety, and a voice that amplifies the things they care about. Someone who wants to tell their story to the world and has something to say.

For the record, it's all branding and reputation, at the end of the day. How your friends, family, coworkers, partners, spouse, investors, customers, and fans experience you *is* your brand. The question is, do you want to create this intentionally and on your terms? Or do you want to let these people or the media come to their own conclusions through happenstance, unconscious assumptions, or even outright lies? I, for one, would like to do my best to ensure I leave people with the impression that I want—in my own words, not someone else's. My family name, reputation, and business depend on it. Yours do too.

Stop Being Invisible

Let's be honest. If you're reading this, right now, you are invisible to the market at large. Nobody really knows who you are, other than your mom and the handful of humans you personally interact with to do what you do. I'm sure they all think you're the bee's knees.

But, therein lies the problem.

Your obscurity is costing you opportunities, money, relationships, and—most importantly—those big dreams you talk about. Whether you're trying to build a human brand or a company brand, if the people you want to reach don't know you exist, well then, you simply don't exist. You're invisible, so to speak.

There are scores of folks in the world offering what you offer, in one way or another, who are less talented, less hard-working, less ethical, or who offer less quality than you do ... but they are doing much better than you are and reaching more people, partly because of their greater visibility. Visibility, notoriety, reputation, and influence will beat the more talented, obscure person all day long. Remember Simona Cattaneo versus Kylie? Simona can run circles around Kylie from a cosmetics business perspective. But Kylie has more influence and much bigger checks, as a result of her notoriety. No disrespect, Simona. You are a boss and crushing it, as far as most people are concerned. And so is Kylie. I'm not mad at Kylie, either. She's doing her thing and winning. Good for her!

How many less talented people with crappier products or services can you point to right now that are dominating your niche? I'm sure you can name a few. They're very annoying.

Truth is, people can't possibly care that you have a great product or service, that you're a nice person, that you truly care about what you do, that you're an expert at your craft, or that you've spent decades working your ass off ... if they don't know you exist.

But, I don't want to be seen as a charlatan!

Brands are not inherently dishonest. Being a person of influence and notoriety doesn't mean you have to become some loud-mouthed, egotistical caricature of yourself. People often feel as though focusing on a personal brand will make them seem like a narcissist or some kind of faker. Those folks are certainly out there, but that's not what I'm talking about here. Let's focus on examples of those you admire who have done it right. That's your target. Build a personal brand you can be proud of. One that can grow as you grow. One that can move from project to project, company to company, without losing credibility. A successful brand will always remain authentic to *you* without ruining your long-term goals in life and business.

Besides: everyone wants to do business with you when you're famous!

I'm being a bit dramatic, but I'm making a point with this statement. It's much more attractive and exciting to do business with someone you've seen in the public eye—a known expert like a published author, celebrity, or business bad-ass whose reputation is known in the space, versus an unknown "nobody."

Ask yourself this question: if you could do business with anyone in the world, is the person who comes to mind a well-known, influential expert? Or an obscure unknown person?

If I was a betting man (and I am), I'd venture to say you chose the former.

I don't need to work on a personal brand; I'll let my merits be my brand!

This is a fair comment. Totally valid position to take. Usain Bolt won eight gold medals in three Olympics, running for less than 115 seconds on the track. He's earned $119 million dollars in the space of ten years, but he was relatively unknown, at first. He became one of the most famous and influential sports figures in the world as a result of his merits. But, for those two minutes, he trained for twenty years.

If you're willing to wait a couple decades to let your results bring you influence, more power to you. If not, I'm with you when you say, *"Ain't nobody got time for that!"*

Personally, I prefer a combination of fast-track brand building along with results-based brand building.

Do I need a personal brand to have a successful business?

Absolutely not! Plenty of businesses crush it without the founder or CEO having a well-known brand.

But, having a personal brand can help your chances of successfully launching a business ... *or,* if you're already running a successful enterprise, a personal brand can most certainly help you be more successful.

Let me prove this to you.

Here's the thing, the world is going to fill in the blanks about you, whether you like it or not. The more they get to know you as a human being, the more you get to control that reputation. The more your fans, followers, customers, and team know you personally, the less likely they will be swayed by outside information that could be harmful to you and your business, whether it's true or not. Having a beloved founder or CEO with a great personal brand can help create a deep brand affinity, driven by fanatical customers who feel personally connected on a whole different level. Think: Steve Jobs, Richard Branson, Elon Musk, Oprah. I heard a brilliant example of this from an incredible young man, business leader, and social media influencer named Steven Bartlett. Here's how he frames the power of a personal brand;

Mark Zuckerberg has hidden in his cave for the last decade and the sentiment around him has even trickled down and had an impact on his stock price over the years. This sentiment has been that he is an evil person who is stealing your data and that he's selling it to people to influence elections. That's the narrative around him. We don't know him, people think he's a robot.

Elon Musk on the other hand has had a personal brand. He's put himself out there in the public domain ,cried on podcasts, smoked weed on YouTube, people think he's an idiot for doing that and they criticise him tremendously, but the thing is with Elon Musk, because he has a personal brand and because I feel like I know him, if the media writes something about him I have my own reference point.

And this is what we call becoming a "glass box." You have a "black box" which is something you can't see inside, they tell you what's inside by painting an image on the outside of it using their PR team or their marketing department or the CEO. Or you have a "glass box" where I can see inside, so I don't need to trust you because I don't trust the PR team anyway, I can see who you are and what you do and how you make your decisions. It allows you to see inside and that builds trust.

– from Steven Bartlett's June 2020 LinkedIn post

I love his "box" analogy. Makes so much sense. Let people see who you are and what motivates you to do what you're doing for the world, and they are more likely to trust you and your company. Shroud yourself in secrecy, stay off the radar, and get ready to cause endless Reddit posts about how you might be part of a conspiracy to ruin the world. Just sayin'!

I would add that Mark has a brand just as much as Elon does; it's just that one is more transparent, honest, relatable, and easier to connect with on a human-being level, while the other is secretive, murky, hard to trust, and doesn't leave you with a sense of who the man is. Both are personal brands. Which one would you rather have in relationship to your business and the public perception?

A Cautionary Tale

I recently read a story about a woman who spent years of her life helping build her company with her co-founder. She and her partner stayed quietly in the background, putting the operation together. As the company grew in popularity, her partner began taking more and more credit for the company's success in the media. Eventually the story in the marketplace was that *he*, and he alone, built this enterprise, and *she* wasn't even a footnote. Imagine dedicating your life to building a company with a partner, trusting that you both will get to enjoy the fruits of your labor, only to be erased from the history books. How can this woman go out and tell the market, "Look, I'm a credible expert founder of this company," when the world only knows about her partner? That guy has built a powerful human brand that he uses to book high-paying speaking gigs, sell his books, get on boards of other companies, attract investors to future deals, and all kinds of other opportunities. Meanwhile, she has to essentially start from scratch, trying to get someone to listen to *her* success story.

Moral of the story? Build your personal brand *now*. Control your narrative.

Okay, fine! I get it. How do I do it?

So, here's the question: how can you *stop being invisible*, take control of your own brand story, and share it with the world in a way that supports what you're trying to project?

This book is all about showing you exactly what you can do to stop being invisible, regardless of what you're up to in the world. Whether you're an executive looking to move up the food chain in your company, an entrepreneur working on a big idea, an artist wanting to grow your fan base, or a business owner with a operation that is currently working well for you ... regardless of where you fit, this information can help you get started on your personal brand. This book will show you some of the basics most people get wrong when putting this knowledge in action.

Let's get to it!

> *Once people know you and trust that*
> *what comes out of your mouth is authentic and true,*
> *it's much easier to get them to listen, follow, subscribe*
> *or even buy from you.*

The Human Brand

Anybody who comes in contact with you or any of your online assets is experiencing your brand. This could be the manager at the grocery store you visit each week, an employer considering you for a job or promotion, a potential mate checking your online profiles before agreeing to a date, your mother-in-law complaining that you're always late, a potential partner or customer considering doing business with you, or an investor checking out how you roll on social media. Your assets include the photos, videos, comments, and articles you post online; your website; your clothes; and the way you speak, just to name a portion of what a brand is. It's *all* connected, and it all reflects how the world sees you.

What do you want people to know about you? How do you want them to feel when they see your website or social channels? How do you want them to feel when they see your image or hear you speak? How do you want people to experience you, no matter how they cross paths with you and your brand?

It all boils down to: *what reputation do you want to have in the world?* Both on and off the court, so to speak. This will determine how you will influence people, your business sector, and the world.

Influence is a megaphone for the lessons, expertise, and experience that only you can bring to the world. You're the only person on earth with your unique story, and there are folks who can relate to the way you did what you did, your philosophies, your perspective. Sadly, many people are afraid to speak up and share their story, in fear they might offend someone or get fired. They're worried they might lose opportunities, or get hateful comments on social media, or that their story isn't good enough.

Let me just tell you right now, your story *is* good enough. *You* are good enough, and someone is out there right now who is in need of your unique voice. You will *never* become an influential human by just fitting in and never speaking up.

And getting a good reception is not always the end goal. The best human brands out there have plenty of haters. Haters are a good indicator that you're doing something right. The flip side is, you'll attract real fans and loyal customers who *love* you and your way of approaching the world.

That means you're going to have to take a public position on something. You'll have to share your perspective on something that has opposing views. You don't have to be a jerk or tear someone else down, but you do have to say something of value and have your own perspective on your niche, industry, and the topics you care about. With so many people saying much the same thing, this is another way you stand out and build a personal brand. Your story, your journey, your experiences, your hacks and tips, your way of approaching and solving challenges that are unique to your niche ... sharing *those* details is how you build a stand-out reputation.

Well, guess what? It's time to make some waves. Because the right people will love you for who you are. But, who is that? Once you get clear on yourself, you can show that self to the world, and shout your messages for the world to finally take notice of. Here's the kicker: folks will actually start thanking you for the honesty.

People long for authenticity and honesty. With so much garbage out there, it's refreshing when a human who is not afraid to share their truth comes along. Especially when it's done with love and good intention. These people always win in the long term. Hey, Gary Vee, I see you, sir! But you can't be authentic and honest if you're not self-aware. You have to know who you are, what you care about, and where you stand before you can start building a human brand. So, that's where we're going to start.

I

SELF-AWARENESS

*The perception others have of you starts
with the perception you have about yourself.
Be aware and deliberate about who you truly are.*

Self-awareness comes first before you even start to craft your personal brand. It sounds simple—knowing who you are and where you want to go—but it is so fundamental that we often don't focus on it. This is a task that can't be overlooked if you want to let others know what makes you tick.

Self-awareness is being able to look inside yourself, check your thoughts, and be honest. It lets you make adjustments when things aren't working out, and take responsibility for the way things are and the way things aren't in your life. It starts by understanding the gears, wiring, and mechanisms inside yourself.

Without this critical component, you won't have a personal brand that's effective, especially long-term—a brand is just not sustainable without this foundational piece being clearly expressed, to yourself first. And this will pay off in other areas of your life. It's actually quite exhausting and miserable not knowing or being your true self. You'll always feel like something is missing. Something is wrong. You'll be left with this slight dissatisfaction with your life all the time. It may go away in certain periods, but it will keep coming back.

You must know yourself. I learned this the hard way. For years, I found myself in weird business partnerships because I wasn't clear about my boundaries, strengths, weakness, etc. It would usually take a year or so before something would go wrong. I would get back up and start again, not really understanding what had happened. I finally took a hard look in the mirror and realized I wasn't being self-aware. I didn't notice I was picking partners and deals for the wrong reasons, unconscious reasons. When I corrected this and got my shit together, my life and business exploded (in a good way).

If you're not checking yourself constantly, being honest about your limitations, setting boundaries, and being self-aware of your motivations, you'll end up in all kinds of crazy places. Over and over, in jobs, relationships, and business deals, you'll constantly be asking yourself, "How the hell did this happen *again!*" or "How did I end up here?" First, you need to know who you are, and what you want (and don't want). If you're aware of your strengths and weaknesses, are clear on your core values, and can communicate all of these things to those around you, it's nearly impossible to end up in places you didn't consciously put yourself into.

Take responsibility. Nobody can do this for you.
And it starts with understanding the mechanisms
and gears inside yourself.

Strengths and Weaknesses

Let's talk about strengths and weaknesses. You need to be clear at what you're great at, and what you're not so great at. See, a lot of people spend time on tasks that are way outside their wheelhouse, and they wonder why they burn time and money and energy trying to achieve something—and it's just because they're wasting time on things they're not great at. So, you need to identify what you do well, and then do that. And do more of that.

You can always fill in the gaps with other folks down the line who can help you in the areas you're not great at. It's called making the right associations and delegating. You can also work on improving in those areas of weakness, but the most important thing is identifying them, so you don't waste your time blindly bumping into walls and wondering why. Get clear first: make a list, write it down. Here's what I'm really, really good at—I can do this in my sleep. Here's the stuff that I just hate doing because I'm not great at it, and the outcomes are never optimal. Be clear on that.

The next puzzle pieces are your values. A lot of folks spend time building a personal brand or building a business that's way out of alignment with their core values. Sometimes it's to emulate another successful person or enterprise; sometimes they just haven't defined their values. Have you ever really sat down and you asked yourself, "What matters to me most?"

I have. For example: things like integrity—doing what I say, when I say I'm going to do it—honor, loyalty... These are things that are nonnegotiable in my life, and if whatever I'm up to doesn't align with those things, I'm not doing it. I cut it out of my life.

Again, these are all components to understanding who you are, so that you can position yourself in alignment with these core identity pieces. This is your self-awareness in the internal world.

Once you're very, very clear on this, then you can start communicating outwardly to the real world, with clarity. Other people respond to this. They can feel your authenticity.

Thoughts, Beliefs, and Feelings

Now, I'm not going to get too deep on this, because this could be a whole book in and of itself. But knowing what thoughts you hold about things—where you stand—will help you shape your message and your positioning. If you don't know what you think, and a lot of the way you behave is unconscious, you're going to end up in places where you're confused, you don't know how you got here. So. you're going to ask yourself, "Man, how did I get here again? How did this happen to me again?" Other people can feel this, too, and it doesn't give them a positive picture of you.

Start with your thoughts. It's very, very simple. We'll put it in a very logical way, so it's easy to understand.

You have a circumstance, right—something that happens—life happens, and then you think things about that circumstance or situation. And then, from there, you feel things about those thoughts. For example, man, you have a job that you're not super excited about, and you start thinking, *God, I just hate this job. I just wish I could do better, and this sucks.*

But when you start thinking like that, you start feeling negative. You start feeling sad. You start feeling regret. All of those negative emotions start coming up. And as a result, you behave a certain way, and you take actions that are congruent with those thoughts and feelings. And then you get outcomes directly related to that whole top-down process.

So, again, I want you to be mindful of the thoughts that you're holding about the things that you're doing, the people in your life; the thoughts you hold about money or about success, marriage, or parenting—whatever they are, you've got to know yourself. You have to know what it is that you're thinking and what you believe, and what it's causing in your life. Get clear on that.

Same thing with your beliefs. There are certain beliefs that you hold. Some are conscious, beliefs that you chose. Some are unconscious, beliefs that you inherited through your family, friends, the neighborhood where you grew up, your faith. This is not about right or wrong, or good or bad; it's just about identifying what you believe and what you think.

This knowledge will help you craft messages that are in line with what really moves you. It will also guide you to cut out the things that no longer serve you, that you may have been holding onto unconsciously, for whatever reason.

I want you to just take a moment. I want you to write these things down.

- Here's what I believe about certain things
- Here are my core beliefs
- Here are the thoughts that I have
- Here's how I feel a lot of times

Get clear on that.

Make adjustments, so you can start thinking and behaving the way that you really want. Intentionally; right? Not on autopilot, not unconsciously.

Passions

When you live with passion, it's infectious. It's like running into that lady who is totally into collecting all sizes and shapes of cool-looking bottles, and when you meet her, she's like, "Oh, I can't wait to tell you about some of the things I'm doing with these funky-looking bottles!" And you're like, "Okay; I don't even collect bottles, but I'm excited too!" And you don't even know why. That's passion.

When people are really passionate about their thing, it rubs off. If you are not passionate about what you're doing for a living or what you're saying to people when you talk about life and the stuff that you're up to, building an effective human brand is not going to happen. It's not going to be attractive to anyone. You need that spark that you can transmit to others. It'll set them on fire too.

Because everybody wants passion in their life. Sometimes it's hard to find. Because most people don't really know what to do, you know? A lot of folks are like, "Well, what do I do? I gotta make a living, and this is just what I know how to do, so I'm going to just keep doing this." Ho-hum. These are the people who end up living a life that's not full of passion, which is sad, because it doesn't need to happen that way if you really think about what you love.

So, take a moment. Think about what you're most passionate about. Don't worry about how you make money with it, or where it will lead you, or what about my friends and family?—don't think about that stuff. I just want you to start to repetitively bring forth the things that you're most passionate about into your consciousness, into your thoughts, and then write them down.

What came to mind? Your first instinct—what are you most passionate about, what lights your fire? Write it down. Okay? Because all this stuff is going to come together in the end to help you figure out how you should present yourself to the world inside of your personal brand.

I want you to think about some of the biggest personal brands in the world, human brands. Think about people, like Oprah, for example, or Will Smith, or Gary Vaynerchuk. These are all people who live passionately. When you watch them, it's infectious, because they're so clear on what they believe, what they stand for, and what their value proposition is to the world. You know exactly what they're up to and what they're trying to cause in the world. Whether you agree with them or not, whether you like them or not, there's no mistaking what they're about when you watch them, listen to them, and consume their content.

I want that same thing from you, and that comes from clarity—internal clarity.

Dreams, Goals, and the Big Vision

So, at this point, let's say that you're clear on why you do what you do, right? As a business and as a person—personally, what gets you fired up.

You know what your strengths and weaknesses are. You know what you should be focusing on, what you do really well. Right? You know what your values are. You know what your thoughts and beliefs and feelings are. This starts to take shape and make sense to you.

Now, what do you want to do with all of that? Where do you want to channel that energy and that clarity? What are your dreams and your big goals? What do you see yourself doing in the world? What would you love to bring to the world?

Whatever those big ideas are, you've got to be clear. Because, again, without a destination, you just kind of float aimlessly. And let's say that you do have some passions you like talking about, and you're clear on your strengths and weaknesses, and you know what your "why " is—but you haven't yet directed it and laser-focused it on a thing, right, on a very clear destination.

Take a moment. Write down what that looks like.

Get rid of all the limiting beliefs, the things like, "Well, I need more money to do that," and "I'd need more time," or "I'm just not smart enough...." Get rid of that stuff for a minute and have fun. Paint a picture of your future. Think:

If nothing was stopping me, if I had everything that I needed, what would I do? What would I do with myself? Where would I direct all of my energy and my passions?

Get clear and write it down. What's the big dream? Maybe you're already building that big dream. If so, this clarity will help you go faster.

Some folks might say, "Hey, I wanna start a program that educates children in Africa." Or some might say, "I want to start a program for pet fostering, right here in my own backyard." Or, "You know what? I just wanna retire and be on a sailboat with my spouse. I just wanna sail around, enjoy the world, and see new things."

Cool. Whatever that is, get clear. Because we're going to tie all this together into a brand position that can help you get there faster.

Just as an example, I want you to think right now of a personal brand, someone—a celebrity or some business mogul that you might follow on Twitter or wherever—and I want you to ask yourself these questions: Why do they do what they do? What is their reason for their business? Why are they even involved in the industry they're in? I guarantee you know the answer, because it's clear; they make it very clear.

Elon Musk, you know him—what is he up to? Why does he do what he does? Why is it that he launched SpaceX and is front man for Tesla? What's he trying to do for the world? You know what his "why" is. It's huge, he's got a gigantic why: he's trying to transform the world with renewable energy, as well as find other planets humanity could live on, in case we continue to screw this one up.

Oprah—I want you to think of why she does what she does. What's she up to? She's up to raising the consciousness of human beings, and getting people to become more self-aware and connected to one another. To love themselves and each other more, so they can enjoy life more.

So think of that, in your mind. Use real-world examples of people you respect and follow, and see if you can answer those questions about those folks: why they do what they do; what they're great at; what their values are; what you think their beliefs and feelings are about certain things that they talk about; what they are passionate about; what their big vision, their dreams or goals are.

I can almost assure you that, whoever you think of, you know some of these answers, just because they're clear. They communicate that in everything they do. It spills out of them, with clarity and that's why you connect with them. You aren't drawn to their brand because it's shiny; you're drawn to their brand because it's a reflection of their core values, and it is that way because they are clear about them.

That's what attracted you to them, that clarity.

You might not know it. You might think, "Oh, I like her show," or "I love the car he makes," but you're actually following that person and connecting to that person and their products because they have clearly expressed their essence. The show, the car—these represent the inner work that they've done, and being able to communicate that with clarity in the marketplace is the mark of a successful brand.

That's really what gets you to buy into Apple. You're clear on their why, you know what they're about. It's what gets people to buy into Tesla. They have a fan base. These are companies that created fanatical users of their products. Even when they go sideways sometimes and make bad decisions, you're connected at a heart level, so you're not going to give up on them.

Virgin's another great example. Media mogul and entrepreneur Richard Branson—you know what he's about. You're clear on what he's up to and what he cares about, and you can see that he cares deeply about his driving forces. And that connects you to him and his company, because he did the inner work, and he communicates what's inside very clearly. It spills over into his companies and his projects. He lives his brand.

That's what I want for you.

Conversely, you can hurt your company by creating a reputation as a company leader that people don't like. We've seen this countless times. Some founder starts piping off on social media over and over again, or does something horrible—like Harvey Weinstein's atrocious, sick behavior— and starts to create a bad reputation which in turn hurts the company. It's all connected.

That's why the self-awareness piece is critical. That's why the human development part is critical. Get this stuff together first. Then we can talk about all the external stuff, the assets and whatnot that go into delivering your message.

And spend some time here. Don't be in such a big rush to move on. Spend some time, because you're doing yourself a disservice if you shortchange this section. Dig in, have fun, really get it fleshed out. Then you'll be on your way to becoming an Oprah or an Elon, not a Harvey.

SUMMARY

A personal brand begins with you, and that means understanding who you are. Self-awareness allows you to take an honest look at yourself. Take responsibility. Nobody can understand you until you do. It all starts with understanding the mechanisms and gears inside yourself.

A personal brand will not be effective or sustainable without self-awareness.

Your "why" is what helps people understand why you do what you do. If you don't clearly explain who you are and what you're about, people won't even know how to interact with you.

WRITE IT DOWN: YOUR "WHY"

What do you do for others? What are some things you offer others, and what is the reason that makes you the person they come to? Examples: You want to fight climate change, or you want to help people understand each other.

WRITE IT DOWN: STRENGTHS & WEAKNESSES

What are your strengths and weaknesses, personally and professionally, internally and externally? List them all out. Take your time here. What are some strengths and weaknesses that others see, that you may not? Examples: being good at art, or being bad at managing your finances.

Remember: Do more of what you're good at. Do less of what you're weak at.

(Pssst… outsource!)

WRITE IT DOWN: VALUES

What values are the most important to you?

My example: Integrity, honor, and loyalty.

WRITE IT DOWN: THOUGHTS, BELIEFS & FEELINGS

If you don't know what you think about things, you're going to end up confused. A lot of our behavior is unconscious, handed down to us by family, friends, and our past experiences. Some of these beliefs are no longer useful to us. Cut them away. Examples: your take on money, citizenship, or relationships.

Remember: You get outcomes directly related to your process.

WRITE IT DOWN: PASSIONS

What are you passionate about? Examples: living to your full potential, freedom, spirituality/religion, helping others, self-improvement, hard work, fitness, health, animals, hobbies, people.

Write down your passions. What puts that fire in your belly?

WRITE IT DOWN: DREAMS, GOALS & BIG VISION

How do your values, beliefs, and passions translate into what you want for your future?

Dion's Example:

I am a personal branding expert, who believes in helping as many passionate entrepreneurs and professionals doing good in the world build influential reputations in their industry. My big vision is to become known as the definitive resource for human brand development. I want to be known as the architect behind some of the world's most impactful human brands. Helping good men and women find, develop, and communicate their truth to the world is my soul's deepest desire and what I believe is my purpose.

As a result, I get to take part in positively changing the world with each person I help break through. My most important values are: family, integrity, honor, loyalty, excellence, passion, caring for others' well-being, creativity, and honesty. I won't give my time to any person or project that doesn't align with these.

My other big goals:

1. Create a global scholarship program, helping people from all over the world and locally have access to free education and training

2. Raise my kids to be happy, healthy, self-confident humans who make noise in the world by doing something positive for humanity

3. Continue to cultivate a deeply connected, juicy, loving, powerful marriage with my best friend and wife; be an example of epic love for our children and the world

4. Win a Grammy for writing a hit song

5. Write, produce, and star in an award-winning movie

6. Build a new kind of school teaching life skills, the arts, and entrepreneurship to kids

7. Write a *New York Times* best-selling book

8. Learn a second language before age fifty

9. Retire my mom

10. Reach nine figures in net worth by my fiftieth birthday

2

STORY DEVELOPMENT

Your experiences have shaped you as an expert in your "thing." Take a closer look at the parts of your story that have molded a one-of-a-kind expert.

This is all about story development, and I'm hopeful that, in the last section, you did all the work and got clear on some of the internal puzzle pieces: the self-awareness, your values, what you believe in, and your strengths and weaknesses. I hope you have some clarity on that, because this story development piece and what's coming after will be a lot more effective and a lot more powerful if that work was done.

So, let's jump right into the story development.

How do you take your life story, your experiences, and expertise, and communicate it in a way that resonates with the folks you want to do business with?

It all starts with writing out your complete, unfiltered life story.

Childhood

I want you to start at the beginning. You're going to go way back: to childhood. I want you to write this down and be very detailed, because no one's going to see this but you, at this stage. I want you to talk about how you grew up, a little bit about your family dynamic, and what area you grew up in. Did you do any moving around and traveling? What were the major life markers that you can remember as kid? Whether these things were positive or negative, whether you feel that it's a pain you don't want to talk about or not, get it all out. Remember, this is for you, and you alone, at this point.

It's important that you add some of this to your story, because it's the real stuff. It's the human experience. When you start getting real and raw and honest about who you are, these are the things that others can relate to. When you try to hide, people can smell inauthenticity, and they know something's not right. Something's missing. So the key here is, you want to have all these pieces in your story. Then we're going to go back, later, and pick out the things that are really most optimal for your brand position. It'll all tie together; you don't have to stress about how it's going to fit together now. Just have a little faith in the process.

So, childhood and family—go back, recall that part of your life, write it all down. Don't edit, judge yourself, or try to look good, at this point. You'll only shortchange yourself in the end.

School Daze

The next piece is your school and education. I want to hear what school life was like for you; from elementary to high school, all the way through college, if you went to college. Let's hear about the experiences you went through. Did you like school? Did you excel at specific subjects? Did you have a teacher who helped or hurt you? Were you bullied? Were you a bully? Who were your best friends? What sort of stuff did you get into? What were the most memorable life markers during your school days? Whatever it is, write it down, talk about the milestones, especially the big, major events that you remember. Even if you think something was uneventful, write it down.

It's surprising to me, when I brand some of our clients, how people tend to gloss over things that may hold real interest for others. When that happens, I'll stop them by saying, "Whoa, whoa, whoa, tell me more about that." And then we both realize that those details are monumental to who they are. It may be a huge turning point or a huge character development point that is often overlooked. A lot of people do it. So, don't edit yourself; write it down and share it all.

Career & Hustle

Let's move on to career and hustle. What did you do when you started moving into the workforce? How was that? Did you immediately go into looking for jobs? Did you take a year off and backpack through Europe? Did you start your first business? What was it like? Did you fail? Did you succeed? What jobs did you try? Write it all down. Talk about your different hustles. Talk about the ups and downs of your adventures in trying to make a living and build an adult life.

Then talk about how you felt. Talk about the thoughts you can remember having along the way, during your most painful and joyful moments. This goes back to some of that self-awareness stuff. I know it's hard to remember, for some folks, because it's been a long time since you've told parts of your story. Or, you may never have told your story at all. In that case, this is a golden opportunity. Take your time and go deep. I promise it will pay off in the end.

Talk about your career pathway or your entrepreneurial hustle and how that went—the ups and downs, and all of the good, juicy details. And I want you to write down the path leading all the way up to today—where you're at right now. Did you walk away from your job and start a small business? Did you find out your start-up wasn't right for you and take a new job? What happened? Tell me about it, and take us up to now, currently. What's going on?

Relationships

The last piece to your story is your history in relationships. This is another critical piece at creating relatedness with humans, because all human beings are in relationships. So, if you leave this part out, you're going to leave out a whole segment of the human experience. Have you been married more than once? Are you dating? Are you single? How's all that going? These are the people who helped you become who you are today. They were part of your growth, your pain, your way of thinking, and so on. How's your relationship with your parents, or whoever raised you—Grandma and Grandma? How was that relationship in the past, and today? Talk about all those relationships in your life. This relationship section is more about you writing out the history of your most memorable personal relationships, from business partners and bosses to lovers and best friends.

Dion's Example: Friendships Shape You

I had a best friend named Matt, and we grew up together. We were inseparable. Summer after summer after summer, we'd hang out together, go to camp, ride our skateboards around town. I learned so much from him. It's funny, I was kind of envious of his life, because he had a mom and dad, and he had a trampoline, and he had a dog, and he had a big house and a yard and a big brother. I, on the other hand, was this little inner-city kid from a broken home, with just me and my mom. It was easy to compare myself to Matt and decide that I had "less" than he did.

As I grew up, I realized that I had this desire to have things look a certain way and felt like a failure if my life didn't match up. I had this attachment to what it's supposed to look like when you have a successful family: mom, dad, dog, kids, yard, trampoline. Once I became aware of this, I was able to ask myself if those things really defined a successful family relationship. When I examined how I really felt, I was able to reframe my model of a healthy family and create a new vision for myself. Now when I do public speaking events, I can talk about the models we create unconsciously that run us well into our adult lives, and how to unpack and rebuild them in a healthy way. It's part of my brand story.

So, look back at your relationships with self-awareness, and consider how they impacted you. What do your past and current relationships mean to you? How do they affect you?

Bonus: Another big thing about taking serious inventory of your life is noticing who's around you right now. Your circle of influence reflects on your human brand (negatively or positively). As you come out the other side of writing out your relationship story, who in your life is reflective of who you want to be and where you want to go in life? Look at your values, dreams, and goals, and see if the people around you help or hinder the realization of your best self.

Maybe it's time to level up your relationships. Maybe you have awesome people around you, and you need to let them know. Only you know the truth.

It's critical that you understand the importance of the rough stuff, the not-so-pretty stuff. A lot of folks tend to focus on the big wins, and the achievements, and the happy stuff because, you know, why do you want to relive your pain? And I get that. But, the painful moments, the stuff that sucks and doesn't feel good, actually forge your character. Adversity is a major contributor to your identity today, in the way you think and the way you approach things. These are all part of your brand, and you want to be able to consciously include them.

So, I just caution you not to gloss over those parts of your life and that part of your story, because it's critical. It's what creates connectedness and relatedness with other human beings, because they get to hear that you're not some perfect, branded person, and you're not some superhero—no one can relate to that. It's hard for anyone to connect when you don't get to see the human side, and the reality that we all struggle through stuff. The key is to talk about what came out of it. Again, self-awareness is a central theme: here's what happened to me, here's some awesome stuff, and here's some of the stuff that really sucked in my life, but I came out the other side much stronger, much wiser. People can either say to themselves, "Wow, that happened to me too," or, "That's so different, but it's something I'd aspire to."

That's connection.

You get it?

Example: Abuse Creates a Protector

A great example is when I first started telling my story, I talked about how I grew up in a single-parent home with my mom. I grew up on welfare for a portion of my childhood. My mom was so awesome: she worked three jobs, and welfare was short-lived. Mom moved us to better and better neighborhoods. I had a wonderful childhood—we laughed, and we played, and it was great.

Well, I left out a critical piece of my life, which was growing up with my mom's abusive boyfriends in my early days. Now some people are like, "Why would you want to talk about that? Nobody wants to hear about it." But people actually do. They either want to know that someone shares their experience, or that someone's different experience contributed something important to their personality and worldview. I discovered, once I started getting real about this, that seeing my mom go through that when I was a little kid created a part of my identity—this protector identity that said, "I wanna make sure this doesn't happen to anyone else." If someone was being victimized or bullied, it became my theme growing up that I'd fight that bully. I'd protect the kid who couldn't protect himself.

How did that spill into my career? Now, I'm the guy that wants to help people find their North Star, find their truth. I want to help them find their authentic self and communicate that to the world, so they can be empowered and go achieve their big dreams. My heart overflows with joy when I can help someone who was afraid to speak their truth finally speak out, or someone who didn't think they were special or worthy unearth their unique superpower and gifts. And so, I found that theme, some of that bad stuff I didn't talk about that actually carried through my entire life into today's career. It made me who I am, and therefore, became part of my brand.

So, think about that for yourself. Spend some time on that piece. Don't leave it out. I promise you, it'll be worth it.

And then, here's a really cool part: I'm going to show you how to tie all that stuff together in the next section: the human, internal, self-awareness stuff— everything that you've been through that led you to where you are today. Whether you're going down a career path or the entrepreneurial path, I'll show you how it all comes together in front-facing assets that actually attract your ideal fan, follower, customer, partner, or investor to whatever it is you're up to.

SUMMARY

Your answers from Section 1: Self Awareness, will help you tell your story. So, how do you take all of that expertise, experience, talent, triumphs, and challenges, and tell that story in a way that makes others want to be a fan or a customer? That's what this section will help you figure out.

Revisit your life and see what stands out. You'd be surprised. So many people ignore some of the most monumental moments of their lives! We all do it.

Write it all down, because it all matters. How did you think or feel at that time? Share what you learned from each of the moments. What did you take from those experiences? What lessons can you share with others?

WRITE IT DOWN: YOUR STORY

Childhood

Let's start at the beginning. How was your childhood and upbringing? The positives and negatives?

Remember: Your life and story are unique to you. There's only one you, and that's what will attract "your tribe," so to speak. Some will connect, and some won't; and that's exactly what you want.

School

Was education important to you? What was your entire schooling like throughout your life? What were the milestones?

Remember: Authenticity is critical. People smell inauthenticity.

Career & Hustle

Let's talk business. What moves did you make? What were your experiences in the real world? Write down all the juicy details of your past hustles and jobs ... all the way up until today.

Relationships

Your personal life and relationships matter. Define and describe your significant relationships in the past and today. Who's in your circle of influence? Family, friends, significant others?

Remember: People don't relate to perfection. Our losses and struggles are what built us today. Don't be afraid to share your faults, challenges, or downfalls. The more you keep it real and share your human imperfections, the more people will connect with you.

3

EXPERT POSITIONING

What is in it for those you are trying to help?
Dig deep into their overall desires. If you help them
avoid a known pain, it's a win-win.

This is where we're going to tell you how to tie all of this stuff together—the work you've been doing so far from Chapters 1 and 2—in a way that's front-facing for the folks outside, to help the fans and the consumer really understand who you are. This is an exciting section for me, because how to position yourself and your brand is something that a lot of folks get wrong, or just simply don't do. You now have a chance to do it right.

It starts with asking yourself some questions and making connections between your answers. I want you to look back at your story and the work that you've done, and I want you to find some themes. This is going to take some self-analysis, but it will show you the constants, or through-lines, in your life. From childhood all the way up through your adult years, you're going to find themes of things that you did, things that you enjoyed, and the kinds of people that you gravitate toward. When you notice those common themes, you'll want to flag them with a checkmark. That's going to indicate who you are naturally—what your disposition and tendencies are.

Look For Themes

The recurring elements of your life and personality are important to know, because they will tie into the next puzzle piece in this section. So, you're going to pull out the themes of your story. Doing this will help you know which parts of your life story can support your brand positioning. They will ensure that your brand is congruent with who you've been, and who you are and where you are currently.

So, I want you to take those themes out.

I also want you to make note of what are you great at, and you can find this information throughout your story. Just be on the lookout for your strengths.

One of mine is public speaking. I've just always been a natural at it. I was known as a "ham" from an early age. I would show up with my mom, aunts, cousins and their friends at a party, and I'd say, "Hey, guys, I have a new joke!" I'd deliver some silly joke, and they would laugh, or I'd sing a song, and they'd clap. They expected it of me. I've always been that kid. Still am.

You'll notice similar themes throughout your life.

You may also notice that there was a way you were for a huge portion of your life, and then you stopped developing that, for some reason. But you were always naturally great at it. Pluck that out, make a note, pay attention; because it may be something you stopped doing due to some kind of trauma, or maybe you went into survival mode. But you may be missing a key element of your passion.

I know for me, there are things I stopped doing because I became a dad, and I let that be the reason why I got a little more practical and stopped being the dreamer who would go for bigger and better things. I got a little more practical for a moment in my life, and I noticed that it just didn't feel good.

Deep down, I felt guilty about losing my passion, and I felt kind of depressed about it. When I recognized this part of my story, by noticing the themes in my life, it brought me up short. I was like, Wait a minute: I've always been *that guy*, and it made me feel alive and passionate and excited. And so, I made the adjustment in my life, and I started going back to my big ideas and reaching for things. Now I'm much, much, happier. I wake up knowing that I get to be who I really am and who I've been for most of my life. I've found ways to bring back this big-idea guy without compromising my family.

And so, I have built up experience in the direction I want to go. I love the business of personal branding. I've learned about idea validation, feasibility work, crafting intelligent business models, proving my assumptions on the cheap, using data to iterate, and partnering with the right people for the right reasons. I'm also ready to say no when things don't match my values, bandwidth, or passions. I've branded myself.

So I want you to pull that out—the parts of your life and your story that are consistent. Take a moment and do some of this now, if you can.... I'll wait.

Okay, so now that you've got an idea of what some of the themes are in your life, hopefully you're more clear on the things that you're great at. I know you can now reflect better on your strengths and weaknesses as well, and you'll probably notice another theme if you compare the two.

Also, think about what you love. What you're great at might not necessarily be what you love, because you've cultivated a skill set and you worked on it, and you became good at something practical that pays the bills and is just what you do. But, compare that to what you love. Can those two things come together? Is there a way for you to bridge the gap between what you love and what you're great at?

Let's hope they're the same things, because that makes it a lot easier exercise. If they are, no-brainer! What you're great at and what you love—these will help you to start to shape your expert positioning in the world. If your work already combines what you love and what you're good at, you're far ahead of most folks and should feel proud of this.

Now let me define expert positioning. As a human brand, your expert positioning is like a value proposition. It says, "Here is what I'm good at and what I do, and here's what that does for folks."

Dion's Example:

I help executives and entrepreneurs clearly communicate who they really are—what they do, why they do it, why they are credible to do it, and who they do it for. We then express that in a way that resonates and heart-connects with the folks they want to attract.

What is it that you love?

What are you great at?

Make the connection between the two.

Once you get clarity on what you're great at and what you love to do, finding out how those two things can intersect can be quite exciting!

Now, I know that some of you might not be able to connect those two things right off the bat, but I promise you there is a way to bridge the gap. When you start to recognize your themes, you'll start to find some answers and some clarity on a way forward. Don't get impatient; just trust the process. Keep playing, keep experimenting and having fun. That will give you a chance to try all this on for size.

The more work you do, the more clarity will come, I assure you.

The other puzzle piece here is, What makes you credible to speak or teach or do the thing that you're great at and you love? The answer is: Your story. What you've been through has forged your credibility. It's your story, and no one else has it. No one can tell you that what you've learned and experienced on your journey isn't valid. It's guaranteed to be your unique edge in the market, because no two stories are the same.

RULE OF BRAND: *Your expert positioning should form a bridge between what you love and what you're great at.*

You're going to pull out the themes from your story that back up or provide evidence of why you're credible to talk about these things. After all, you are an expert on you.

Example: Bullied into Confidence

A man we'll call "Eric" was bullied as a kid, and he did not enjoy his school upbringing. And then, when he got to college, he met a professor who helped him develop confidence and self-esteem by kind of unpacking some of the damage from when he was a little kid. He thought, *Man, imagine if kids had this same sort of training when they were young, at that same age when he was bullied.* And so, Eric went on a mission to master all of the things that his professor taught him. And over the next ten years, he developed an expert knowledge base on how to work with children to help them have self-esteem and confidence when they're younger.

As you can see in that story: the guy went through it, he solved his problem, and then he equipped himself to teach what he'd just learned. *That's credible.* Now Eric has a business teaching young kids in a way that develops their self-esteem and confidence. You get the point? Look at your story and find what makes you credible to talk about the things you want to talk about. It could be your formal education, your family upbringing, childhood experiences, in-the-trenches training, business adventures, etc.

Let's say that you're struggling to connect what you love with what you're great at. Consider what you can use from your history to show that, "Hey, I'm credible: I'm knowledgeable, and I'm good at this." Maybe you don't have all the chops to make you an expert on what you want to talk about or share with the world. That's totally okay. That doesn't make you a fraud. You just have to be honest with people, and keep it real. You can get your foot in the door by sharing on social media your unique *viewpoint* about it. Say, "Here's a thing I love. I'm really good at it, but I'm new to it." Be honest. People appreciate that kind of humility, and you can develop more credibility over time.

Eventually, you'll look back after you've been doing this for a year or so and say, "Hey, I've been putting in my ten thousand hours on this.... Now I can say that I'm credible, because I've been putting this out on the market and being honest with people." Authenticity, honesty, and integrity will make all the difference.

Your expert positioning is not just the value proposition, meaning it's not just, Here's what I do, here's who I serve, here's why I'm credible to do this thing, build this business, teach this course, or whatever it may be. There are other components.

One is who you want to attract. It makes a difference. Who are you talking to? You need to get clear on that, too, because that will determine some of the little fine-tuning and tweaks that you do to your positioning, to make sure that you're actually getting through the filter of those folks.

Here's a great example: let's say that, for your positioning, you really want to speak to eighteen to twenty four-year olds. Okay? But, all of your language is written to fit more of a forty- and fifty-plus perspective. You might be credible to talk to teenagers and young folks, but your message doesn't get through because you haven't refined and tweaked the language to fit that audience. And a lot of people get this wrong. They wonder why they don't attract the right folks.

A lot depends on how you're saying it. Are you delivering a message that fits that group? And are you sending that message to the correct watering holes where those folks are? Print newspapers, for instance, might reach the forty-fifty crowd, but the younger demographic just won't be there. You'll still be invisible to them. So, get super, super clear on who that group is, in order to tweak your messaging in the right direction.

Warning: don't try to be something you're not, though, just to relate to a certain audience. This is a tricky one. It's like the older dad trying to be cool for his teenage kids and their friends. It's cringey and weird. Be yourself, but learn the cadence, topics, and language of the audience, and figure out how to be in on their conversation in your own way.

The last puzzle piece to your expert positioning is this: once you're clear on who you're talking to, what you're saying, what you're great at, and what your value proposition is ... now you've got to figure out what is the best way to get this message out there.

Is it through the written word? Is it through audio or video? Is it live presentations? Is it all of that?

This is where you have to do some more self-analysis. It comes back to self-awareness. Maybe you're terrible on video. You're just not a video person. That could actually hurt your brand until you develop that skill set. So, the initial strategy should be to use the distribution methods that fit your natural skill set. If you're a great writer, write—write blogs, LinkedIn posts, Medium articles. Take advantage of all the different places you can go to distribute the written word.

If you're great on video, well, that's cool. It's a bonus, because you can piggyback off of it to spin more content. You can record and post videos, and then transcribe the audio from those into blog posts. Once you have a number of blog posts together, you can fashion them into a speech or even a book.

But whatever it is, be honest about your strengths. This will let you build your brand from a really solid, comfortable foundation that doesn't force you to work outside of your wheelhouse initially. You can push yourself and stretch later; those things are more difficult when you're building. And then, over time, you can develop the skills to do other forms of distribution.

With this new clarity on your expert positioning, your story, and your internal self-awareness, you're good to go. All of this will now come together smoothly in creating the front-facing assets that you'll use as vehicles to get your message out there.

SUMMARY

Your expert positioning ties everything together for your audience, so they can understand who you are—quickly and clearly.

Take a look back at the work you've done in the earlier sections. What themes emerge? Take a step back and really look at the story objectively. You'll notice that some themes keep popping out. If an action, occurrence, attitude, or anything in your story happened numerous times, we'll call that a theme.

These themes will help identify some of the things that come naturally to you. Did you find any?

WRITE IT DOWN: THEMES

What themes emerged? These are the things that probably come naturally to you, whether you've thought about it that way or not. Now, let's revisit your Strengths & Weaknesses exercise from Section 1.

Again, write down what you are great at.

Compare your strengths and themes. Do the two match up? You may notice that you strayed from what came naturally. A lot of us do for many different reasons. Often, we don't think it's practical to continue doing what we're most comfortable with. It's okay! That's natural!

Do your strengths and themes support the positioning you want to take in the world? Which parts of your story are consistent with these? Answering these questions will help you clearly define your expert positioning.

What do you love to do? Is there a commonality between what you love and what you are great at? Keep these answers in your head, because you're going to need them for creating your value proposition.

Your expert positioning is made of three components.

Expert Positioning

1. Value Proposition

2. Audience

3. Method of Delivery

Let's get that first piece down.

1. Value Proposition

The first prong of your expert positioning is your value proposition. To put it simply, your value proposition should say, "This is what I'm good at and what I do for others. This is how it will benefit you."

Dion's Example: I brand humans and their big ideas and help them get clarity, so they can move the needle on what's important to them by having a voice and reputation in their industry that matters.

Remember: Connect what you love and what you do.

Are you comfortable owning that value proposition? Remember the bullying and confidence example? Parts of your story will support your expertise.

Which parts of your story support or align with your "thing"? Which parts of your story make you credible to teach what you know or do what you do?

If you're struggling to connect the dots, that's okay. Just be honest with your audience. Share your journey, and people will appreciate that honesty. After a while, you will have the experience to back it up!

Remember: Honesty and passion are attractive.

Next, let's review who will receive your message.

2. Audience

Who are you talking to? Who do you want to attract? Get clear on that first, to make sure you're getting through their filter. Ask yourself who is most likely to be excited by what you have to say. In other words, who is most likely to find your value attractive?

Example: Missing the Target

Let's say you're targeting people between ages eighteen and twenty-four, but your language is written for an older audience. You might be credible, but your message isn't going to get through. Get clear so you know how to tweak your presentation.

Remember: Your tone and language must be consistent with your target audience *and* authentic to you. It also must be congruent across your entire brand. Don't try to be one thing over here and another thing over there. When your audience finds out, you'll lose trust.

Now that you've got the "what," and the "who," let's review the "how."

3. Method of Delivery

Once you're clear on what you're going to say and who you're saying it to, you need to identify the best way to get your message to your adoring public.

Written word? Audio? Video? Live?

Which methods feel comfortable to you? Use those that fit your natural skill sets. Play to your strengths and build a strong foundation. Over time, you can build on your weak areas.

Also, consider which methods your target audience wants to consume. Do a little market research on your demographic so you'll know which way to go.

4

WEBSITE

Your website is your home base. Your headquarters.
Your digital living room. Invite your audience in to spend
some time with you, and make it enjoyable for them.

Wiggity-wiggity-wiggity-wiggity-website

It's time to put together all of the front-facing assets that represent your human brand. We're going to start with what I call your "home base." This is where everyone will come to visit you and listen to what you have to say. It's your central hub, and it's your website. Now, some people might think websites are going away, that they're not important; but it's actually just the opposite. The Web is the one constant that will always be relevant, will always be up-to-date, and—most importantly—will always be controlled by you.

The social channels and other platforms that you might use change constantly. You don't fully control them, so you're limited by their platform, their format, their rules, their politics and regulations, and whatever changes they make to their business model. Social channels can censor your views, block your content or ban you completely if your views don't match their own. Your home base—your website—is the one place where you can control the narrative completely.

So, let's make it very clear: do not shortchange yourself on your site. This is where you want to take people. This is your home. This is where they learn about you, on *your* terms: they'll learn about your projects, the things you care about, your ethos, and what you're up to, all presented in their best light. Once they're engaged, they can find out how to contact you, plus all the different social channels where they can follow you.

Let's start with an understanding of the importance of your website's format and layout. These will create a first impression of your brand, as well as the type of connection that leads to conversion. "Conversion" means converting a passive audience into an interactive one. They come onto your site, and you get a desired behavior from them. If you want them to like something, or follow you, or check out a book that you wrote, check out a podcast, or subscribe to your newsletter, the presentation and message you project will encourage them to do those things.

The desired outcomes that you're trying to drive will determine how you shape your website, so that you make your point with complete clarity. It's not just about aesthetics and the site being pretty, which is fine if that matches your brand. It is about the total package that is meant to convert that traffic in a meaningful way.

But there are some hard and fast design principles that will help you cement that first impression. One is the initial screen image. As soon as people pull that up—*Bam!* The first thing they see is the stuff placed "above the fold," or what's called the "hero" position. You need to make sure that everything above the point where they actually have to scroll and take an action is clear and drives them to the next place. It should immediately convey where they've landed, why they're there, and what's next—what you want from them.

The "above the fold" view looks different on different devices. So, you should always be building your site with mobile in mind first, because most of your users are going to come from their mobile phones. From there, you can take into account different screen sizes and devices. So, building a site the right way is not just point-and-click. You actually have to go on there and do the work to tweak it and make sure it looks optimal on various devices, which is no easy feat. But it can be done with some persistent effort.

So, let's talk about "above the fold " for a moment, and what that actually means, as well as which components you should have in that critical real estate. The first thing is some kind of a headline. Who are you? Why are your viewers there? Maybe they land right on your site, and they see your beautiful face along with a headline that says, *I teach people how to cook healthy meals from home.* Ah—*bam!* They know exactly what this site is about. Or, *I help authors publish their first book.* Got it. A headline should encompass a very concise value proposition, so that viewers know where they're at, why they're there, and what's happening. This plays into your brand by showing them that those things are a reflection of *you.* You've just added to your human brand.

So, your headline should be concise and tell folks they're in the right place. The rest of your site should clearly and simply demonstrate how to access what they came for.

Now, scroll down. It's time to take an action. Pretend you are a first-time viewer. How do you want them to experience your website? What do you want them to take away? Do you want them to go to the bottom of the page and consume everything on the way down? All of these details will combine to create the user experience. It should be effortless and engaging. And the content? You want to tell a very compelling story all the way through that has them eager to go:

to the next piece,

and the next piece,

and the next piece.

You've surfed the Web. There are a lot of confusing websites out there. Some have all kinds of exit points, words everywhere, random colors, multiple logos and tag lines, too many things people can click on, tons of social links.... More is not always better. With too much going on, it's hard for users to understand the value proposition. They get frustrated. *What do you want from me? What do I do here?*

Make that experience very simple and clear by focusing on your desired behavior. What do you want your audience to do? That comes in the form of your copywriting; what is your message? What story are you telling? What words are you using? Where are you leading viewers?

Then, think about how logical your navigation tools are. They should be obvious and succinct. Are there a dozen links at the top of your page or down the side that are distracting? You're better off keeping navigation simple, so that users don't get confused, click around looking for what they really want, and eventually leave. And links to outside websites? Are you kidding me? Just say no.

And then, another critical component is a call to action. This engages viewers by inviting them to do something: "Join my newsletter." "Subscribe for tips and tricks." "Follow me here." "Do [fill in the blank]." If you don't tell people what to do, they just kind of willy-nilly navigate around your site and then leave.

Give them helpful and inviting instructions.

I want you to also be aware of the imagery that you're using on your site: the sizing, the spacing, and the priority that you place on each photo or line drawing. How much real estate do you really want to take up with a picture of your cat? That might not be optimal for your brand, unless you have a cat-sitting business. The page might take a long time to load because of the gigantic photo, and then people have to scroll to get past it, to find anything meaningful. While the cat picture might reveal your personality, consider what's most important to the *viewer*, and let that guide your priority placement.

As you build the site, be aware of that stuff. Look at it. Test it on different devices. How many actions does a user have to take before they get to the heart of the matter or locate what they came there to see? You want minimal actions between that first impression and user satisfaction.

Consider this: every action I have to take reduces the likelihood of a conversion. But the conversion should not drive the total experience. You have to add value to your request for action.

Sure, you could create a site that's just designed to convert for one particular thing, but that's not a very nice user experience. If it's all about "buy my thing," people who aren't ready to buy will go away. So, you'll lose some folks there. If there's nothing else for viewers to do but buy the product, or subscribe to your newsletter, they'll feel, well … used.

That is not the emotion you are going for on your home page; there's got to be more. It's about telling your story. It's about inviting them in. You want them to get to know you. *Then* ask. Then they'll be more likely to convert.

SUMMARY

Your website is your home base.

Websites will always be relevant, and they are controlled by you. Other social channels and platforms change constantly over time—in relevance and popularity. That makes your website as important as the house that you live in ... or a close second, anyway.

Remember: You control the narrative of your website. You get to choose how you want the world to see you.

Your website is the one place that anybody in the world can find you and contact you *for the rest of your life.* So, the format and layout of your website is critical. Because most users come from mobile phones, always design with mobile in mind, first!

Aesthetics are important, but there are some other core principles that will help you convert traffic in a meaningful way. You need to make it clear what action you want viewers to take. And express it in a way that makes them really, really want to do that.

Remember: Look at sizing and spacing of images. Don't let them be distracting and get in the way of the desired action.

Above the Fold is the most eye-catching real estate on your website; it includes everything above the point at which your audience has to scroll. Your headline should clearly tell people who you are and what's in the website for them. A headline is like a very concise value proposition. It can also include some personality. Get creative or hire a pro.

The headline should say who you are and why viewers should care. What's in it for them? A headline is a very concise value proposition.

Examples:

"I teach people how to cook healthy meals from home."

"I help authors publish their first book."

The headline should let people know they are in the right place, if they are looking for someone like you. Once that is established, they'll continue on, wherever you direct them to go.

So, it's up to you to lead them where you want them to go!

How do you want users to experience your website? What do you want them to take away? Eliminate any confusion by making the experience simple and clear, focused on the desired behavior you want them to do. If they get confused, you'll lose them.

How many actions does your user have to take to get them to the next step? You want them to take minimal actions. The more actions they take puts them farther away from a conversion. Your words, links, and navigation must be simple and must direct your audience to wherever you want them to go.

Once they get there, it's time to be even more direct. You need to make it clear what action you want them to take. The **Call to Action** should tell your audience exactly what to do.

Remember: Building a website for conversion is *not* enough. Invite your audience in, make them feel comfortable, and give them something of value—your content—just for being there.

5

SOCIAL CHANNELS

Choose channels you're comfortable with.
And be yourself consistently.

In this section, we're going to talk about social channels and the nuances between the types of channels. So, while you're deciding which of the social platforms are best for you, you'll have a really good framework and a definition for how each one can be leveraged.

The best way to determine which channels you should focus on is based on the type of content that you're comfortable creating. Also, consider where your ideal audience consumes content. For example, if you're a writer, and you know you're great with the written word, you can focus on the blog piece. You can focus on Twitter, because it's a written format in which you can technically have conversation drops and quotes, and interact with people via writing. It's a great platform for that.

So is LinkedIn. LinkedIn's ideal for that, since you can drop whole articles there. A number of other platforms, such as Medium and HuffPost, are best for longer articles, if that's what you like to write. Go with the platforms that you're really going to use and that fit your most comfortable distribution type.

A lot of people link every channel under the sun to their websites, because they're like, "Oh, I should have them all." Yeah, maybe … if you're going to use them all. It's a better to position yourself via channels that you're active on rather than vacant channels. If someone comes across your Instagram channel and you just don't use it—let's say you have, like, one photo on there—it's probably not optimal for your brand positioning.

"Why isn't this person active?" they'll wonder. Maybe they don't go to your other channels, they just go to that one; now they think that you're not an active poster, they think that you're someone who doesn't care about your channels, that you're outdated, or are not a real person. Depending on what your business is, this could be very harmful. Misrepresentation can actually be *worse* than invisibility.

So, I would get rid of channels you're not going to use or are not using. You can always add them later, as you become more proficient in the different types of content strategies.

Suppose you're very comfortable with video. Well, that'd be a good opportunity for you to start a vlog, much like a blog, but it's video. And there are a few distribution channels or social channel platforms that are perfect for the video maker. Instagram's great for the short content, the teasers, quick tips, and little rants. These things could set you up for longer-form video that you might host on YouTube or Facebook.

YouTube is the go-to platform for longer form video. For example, your YouTube vlog might be your daily hustle: you're checking in with people, you're showing them what you're up to, you're going over here for a lunch meeting, you're in the studio recording a podcast. Whatever, you're showing them your day. People start to subscribe and follow you, they tell their friends, and the videos really pay off.

RULE OF BRAND: *Long-form video makes great micro content that you can chop up, repurpose, and use everywhere!*

You can chop that into whatever size video you want on YouTube, for people to see the whole picture, but then you can also chop that up into mini content that you can leverage on a channel like Instagram, for example. It works both ways.

Or you can put little teasers on there and say, "Hey, for the full video, come to my YouTube channel." So, that's a great content piece and a great channel for those who like video.

For deeper information on how to leverage each channel, there are a ton of resources online. Make sure you research the platform so you understand the nuances, because you can actually hurt your brand by leveraging a channel the wrong way. You might put the wrong type of content on there, only to find that your target audience doesn't frequent that channel for that type of content. You need to know the difference in viewer demographics and how to optimally use each platform.

It's also important to be congruent across all the channels that you're going to use. So if you're using Twitter, Facebook, YouTube, and Instagram, make sure that no matter which channel someone goes to, they see the same brand positioning. It's the same expert positioning. You don't want your business philosophy coming through on one site and just a big picture of your cat on another.

In other words, don't cause confusion. This happens when someone finds you on one channel, subscribes to you, and believes in what you said you are ... and then, on another channel, you flip the script on them and present yourself as something completely different. That will actually hurt your brand. You can start losing followers and fans that way. So be consistent.

Each channel has its own specific branding opportunities, as well. For example, on YouTube you can do headers and profile pictures. You can have an intro video when someone lands on your channel, of whatever you want them to see first. Make sure you understand the different branding opportunities.

Also, make sure your descriptions are the same, no matter where someone finds you. So whatever it is you're saying about yourself, however you want to position yourself—make them the same everywhere. That's brand congruence.

SUMMARY

Before digging into the huge world of social media and its various channels, we need to establish what type of content you'll be focusing on. Social channels have different functions and capabilities that make them better suited for different types of content.

Where are you most comfortable? With the written word? In front of the camera? Or is your voice your golden ticket? Pick what's natural for you. You don't need them all. Use channels you will be active on, so you can establish and maintain your presence.

Remember: Make sure your descriptions are the same across all of your channels.

Here's a quick summary of some of the most popular channels.

Facebook

Facebook houses a vast array of capabilities, such as a marketplace, public/private groups, and communities. It is also becoming the largest medium for advertising worldwide, offering unequaled precision audience targeting. You can have numerous profiles—personal, public figure, business, and groups. This platform allows you to share images, videos, text, and live video stream.

Instagram

Instagram allows users to share content with their followers via photos, short videos, and chat. The Instagram Stories feature lets you provide a snapshot of periods of time with a connected snapshot of moments via images, text, video, and audio. This is the perfect feature for sharing real-time photos and videos, especially for project and product launches and events. Each post can include a maximum of thirty hashtags, which can be used to promote your message and group it with other relative topics, to connect with different audiences.

Twitter

Successful brands often use Twitter to share links and smaller bite-sized messages to drive people to longer-form content, such as their sites or blogs. The platform also allows you to upload images and live streams. Hashtags are prevalent on Twitter to help users filter conversation and topics, and group posts with other relevant topics.

LinkedIn

LinkedIn is where your professional online presence lives. Known as the professional network, LinkedIn allows users to showcase their resumes, accolades, and portfolio to attract employers, employees, investors, business partners, and peers. This platform is the one place where your professional network can find your personal brand, expertise, experience, training, education, credibility, and references.

YouTube

YouTube's free video-sharing community allows users to create profiles and video content for building their brands and sharing their expertise. YouTube is the number-one source for video content. It is the world's second-largest search engine and third most-visited site after Google and Facebook. Users can: upload and monetize their own content; watch, like, and comment on other videos; create content playlists; and livestream.

Vlogs and video make great micro-content that you can use everywhere!

Chop up your vlog into any size video to post on YouTube, and chop that up even smaller for mini content that you can leverage on other channels. Use the mini-content to drive people to the longer form videos.

Example: "For the rest of the video, visit my YouTube channel."

Remember: Each channel provides distinct and specific branding opportunities.

Social Media Image Size Cheat Sheet

When it comes to photo and video, each channel comes with different requirements and sizes. It's important that you understand the differences and the preferred formats for each. At the time of this writing, the following sizes look great on each platform. You'll have to periodically check to see if anything has changed on specific platforms, to ensure your branding still looks as you intended.

Facebook

Profile Picture: 180 x 180 (Displays 170 x 170 on Desktop)

Cover Photo: 820 x 312

Shared Image: 1,200 x 630

Shared Link: 1,200 x 628

Highlighted Image: 1,200 x 717 (Recommended)

Instagram

Profile Picture: 110 x 110

Photo Thumbnails: 161 x 161

Photo Size: 1080 x 1080

Instagram Stories: 1080 x 1920

Twitter

Profile Photo: 400 x 400 (Displays 200 x 200)

Header Photo: 1,500 x 500

In-Stream Photo: Minimum 440 x 220 (2:1 Ratio)

YouTube

Channel Profile Image: 800 x 800

Channel Cover Photo: 2,560 x 1,440

Tablet display: 1,855 x 423.

Mobile display: 1,546 x 423.

TV display: 2,560 x 1,440.

Desktop: 2,560 x 423 (1,546 x 423 pixels are always visible).

Video Uploads: 1280 x 720 (Minimum HD)

LinkedIn

Personal Profile Image: 400 x 400 (Recommended)

Personal Background Image: 1584 x 396

Company Logo Image: 300 x 300

Square Logo: 60 x 60

Company Cover Image: Between 1536 x 768

6

PERSONAL STYLE

Don't lie! We all judge others based on first appearances.
It's what they see before you open your mouth.

If I asked you what a wealthy, successful businessperson looks like, does a certain style come to mind? What clothes do they wear? What hairstyle do you see? Do they wear certain jewelry? What car would this person pull up in? What else do you imagine, visually, when you think of a successful person?

We all know that successful people come in all shapes, sizes, styles, and ethnicities. But each of us carries an initial knee-jerk, unconscious (and conscious) assumption about what certain visuals mean, even if our first-hand experiences contradict these assumptions. Many of these biases were planted in our brains unbeknownst to us from our family, neighborhood, culture, religion, Hollywood movies, TV shows, and brilliant marketing agencies trying to sell a product.

With each person on the list below what do you see in your mind?

Rapper

Valley Girl

Pastor

CEO

Real Estate Agent

Doctor

Politician

Beach Bum

Professor

Tech Company Founder

Outdoorsman

Girl Next Door

Millionaire

Nerd

It's pretty easy to come up with an initial visual in your mind of what each of these types of people might look like, if you don't overthink it, even knowing that there are huge visual variances in the real world. There is a general agreement between humans on what these "characters" should look like. Ask a hundred people, and you'll probably get a large majority who agree on what a CEO should look like. I'll bet they say a suit and tie are part of the outfit. The nerd obviously wears glasses. These archetypes or characters are pervasive and are usually cemented in our minds. Thanks, Hollywood! Thanks, Madison Avenue.

So, this begs the question, what do people see when they look at you? Is your visual presentation in line with who you are telling people you are? When there's a mismatch between how you represent yourself visually and what you say you are, it causes dissonance in the minds of your audience on an unconscious level. This is a huge problem, because folks might not even know why they don't trust you, or they might lump you in with an entire group of people solely based on the familiar bias in their minds.

No one wants to remind people of the sleazy, pushy used-car salesman. But if you dress like that dude, you might unknowingly be creating this association in the minds of people considering doing business with you. If you want to communicate that you are a high-end, refined professional, you might want to rethink your Instagram posts of you dancing in your underwear. If you're telling folks you're the down-home country boy, but in your Facebook photo you're standing next to a Bentley in a five thousand–dollar Armani suit, you might confuse some folks. And confusion reduces trust. You do you, if it's authentic and you're clear on who you're trying to attract.

Learn which archetype you might be associated with. Then, either change your visual presentation to match it, or change your brand positioning if you don't like the association. Alternatively, you can do whatever the heck you want, but address it so your audience knows you're aware you don't fit the mold. The Silicon Valley tech folks have definitely broken the suit-and-tie CEO mold. The whole point here is awareness and intentionality. If you know what you're doing and why, then you are in control of your brand.

Don't match the archetype you want to project? For those that need it, I'm going to share a few pointers that will help you dial in your personal appearance. There are some basic theories and principles that I want to relate that will help you understand how humans perceive style, clothing choice, and color pairings. I'm going to run you through a couple of the basics, just so you can get your mind around how this works.

Color Pairing

When you're looking for what kind of shirt to get and how it should look in relation to the rest of your wardrobe, you need to be aware of fabric colors in relation to your hair color, your eye color, your skin tone. First, you need to be know that certain color pairings just don't work.

For example, if you're really dark, wearing brown or other dark-colored clothing is not optimal. There's no pop to it. It blends with your skin. It looks like a skin suit. It just doesn't work, and you need to shy away from those tones, even if you really like them. When the visuals are wrong, people will not be attracted. They might not know why, but it's hard to look past the visuals to what's on the inside when colors are out of whack. They're the first things you see.

Think about your top-line brand positioning. Your style is part of your entire brand ecosystem. It all communicates the same thing. It all tells the same story about you; and so, if you want to look like a polished professional, like a serious businesswoman or businessman, you need to dress accordingly. Like I said before, there are some unconscious agreements among humans by way of Hollywood, film, television, and big brands. They've already shaped our minds on what a successful business person looks like. You can either fight those stereotypes and try to be different, or go with the flow and make getting brand acceptance a bit easier for yourself.

I, for one, pay attention to the basic expectations of humans when it comes to putting together a look, instead of going too far outside the box. At the end of the day, though, your goal should be to do what you have to do to get your message across, so long as you don't compromise who you are. Sure, sometimes you do need to stretch yourself beyond your comfort zone. There's a time to level up your gear. Wearing a T-shirt and jeans all the time just because you don't have the patience to go shopping, though, is no reason to keep your brand from evolving. It might be time to grow up and work on your look. The other thing is, a well put-together style communicates to folks that you probably treat your business with the same level of care and attention. That's a powerful assumption to create in the minds of your audience.

When a well-dressed person with a little style walks into a room, they get attention. When that person has good energy, is confident, and can share what they do with clarity and passion, they can literally own the room.

I want this for you!

If you don't want to put on a suit, you don't have to wear the tie; you can "cool it up" a little bit. But if you're trying to say, "My brand is a credible professional, and I'm trying to attract corporate leaders to my consulting business,"— but you dress like a rock star in a leather jacket and torn jeans—it might not work. You might not attract that group. You have to be aware of your clothing and how that is communicating your brand.

Yes, there are no rules in art. In fashion, you can represent yourself however you want, and you can be free as a bird. But remember what it is that you're trying to communicate. Start with the fundamentals of color pairing. Know that there are basic human agreements on which colors go together.

Here's a great example: you're walking down the street with your friend, and you see a big, purple truck with pink rims, gold trim, and red seats. It literally assaults your eyes. You're going to look and go, "What in the heck just happened?" That jumble of colors doesn't work. Now, if you're *wearing* something like that, it stands out—but it probably isn't something that's going to attract people to you in a positive way, unless you're a performance artist of some sort.

In any other business, the clown look won't cut it. That's how people think of you when you have wild color pairings that just don't make sense for most humans and the agreements we all have about which colors go together nicely.

Shopping

So, how do you find the colors, cuts, and fabrics that look well on you and add to, not detract from, your professional image? Well, you can experiment and practice. Or you can consult someone who has an eye for fashion design.

RULE OF BRAND: *Find someone who is into fashion to help you. Most people would love the opportunity! Students and young, eager professionals can always use a testimonial, reference, or portfolio piece.*

Here's my suggestion for those who feel like they're a little fashion-challenged and can't seem to get a look that they love: find a personal shopper or a stylist. No matter where you live, somebody in your town will have a great eye for fashion and how to dress people. If you're in a city that has Nordstrom, for instance, you can access personal shoppers and stylists on-staff ... not just a person at the register. Just ask about the service and say, "Hey, I'm interested in having one of your personal shoppers help me pick out some outfits."

Or, you can find your local boutique fashion stores—those are typically started by folks who have a deep love for fashion. They may have a good sense of design and how to dress. Pop in there and see if there's someone who can help you put together a look.

Whatever you do, be open to experimenting. You don't have to buy it, and you don't have to walk out of the store with it. But, try it. I know some of you are like, "Nope, I'm always going to wear my cowboy boots, you can't get me out of them." I respect that. But it won't hurt you to be a little adventurous with this. You might land on something you never thought you'd wear but find out you look incredible in. That makes you feel incredible, which builds your confidence, which translates directly to a strong brand.

It won't cost you a cent to try on a new look. Don't be afraid to look at some outfits, take some photos, and then bring those back to people you respect and trust to get their feedback. "Hey, I went and tried on some stuff. I wanted to try a new look. What do you think?" Their impressions will help you make a decision.

Now, if you live in a small town and you don't have any little boutiques that you would shop at, or you don't have a

Nordstrom or whatever, this is a little trick or hack that you can use that might work. It depends on who's in your town. But you could even do something like post on Facebook or do a little Craigslist ad that says, "I'm looking for someone in my town that has a great fashion sense, that understands these types of things, that understands that I'm trying to look like this. I'm trying to model myself after this kind of look." You'll be surprised: there's most likely someone in your town who has a great eye and would love to help you out.

The most important takeaway from this section is to understand how important your personal style is to your brand positioning and the overall brand ecosystem of you. It all ties together, from your website design to your photos and videos ... from the colors you choose and the way that you dress to how you communicate. It's all part of the same system.

If one piece is incongruent, it can create mistrust unconsciously in the minds of those who are checking you out.

Just know that they might not tell you, but for some reason, you can tell things just aren't working. There's probably a piece that is incongruent and breaking the ecosystem. Just be aware that it all counts.

A great example that I want to share with you is one of my dearest, beloved clients, Dr. T. He came to us with a vision of growing his brand and awareness online as a digital marketer. He was kind of stuck in his practice as a doctor. He couldn't really earn any money unless he was at his practice every day. He wanted to explore how to take his knowledge and monetize it online. So we said, "Okay, tell us who you want to attract." He replied, "I want to attract professionals and high-income earners... people that are like me, who do really well in the real world but who want to move out into a more leveraged income opportunity."

So, we asked to review his wardrobe and how he paired pieces of it. Remember, he wants to attract high net-worth earners, folks who are successful like he is, professionals—and here's how he dressed.

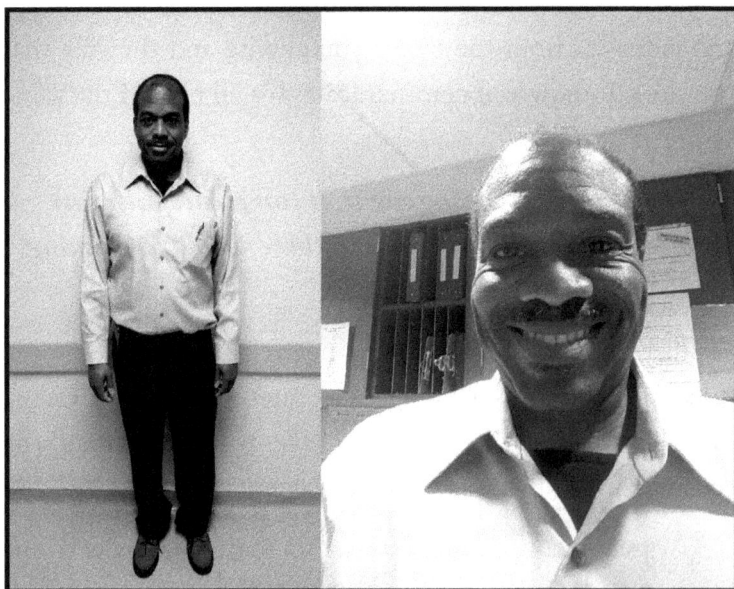

Now I want to show you what happened when we worked with him, and he made some adjustments to his wardrobe and his appearance. Look at the difference.

Do you see what I mean?

It's a profound difference. It made all the difference in his brand positioning, and it set him on a new path. He lit on fire after this, by the way. You can tell what that would do for his confidence, his self-esteem, and his ability to project a more proactive image, which suits him well in his new business.

I want the same thing for you, so be mindful of how powerful this image piece can be.

SUMMARY

The way you dress and present yourself are critical. Here are some basic principles to help you look your best. Your style is part of your brand ecosystem, and your clothing should align to your overall expert positioning. Your style is just as important as any brand asset. It all ties together. If one element of the ecosystem sticks out, it can be detrimental to your entire brand.

A new personal style can give you so much confidence, though. It can make you feel incredible!

Color Pairing: You need to be aware of the relationship between colors and your personal attributes—your hair color, eye color, and skin tone. All these things matter.

Remember: If you don't have fashion sense, find someone to help you.

- Personal shopper
- Stylist
- Department stores
- Boutique fashion stores
- Experiment
- Post on social for a shopping buddy

Style Guide Quick Tips

How to choose the right colors for your face/skin tone: A general rule of thumb is that warm colors look good on warm skin tones, and cool colors look good on cool skin tones.

Warm skin tones can vary from yellow to peach, beige to warm brown, reddish-brown to deep brown, and many shades in-between.

Cool tones can be white, pink, pinkish-red, deep dark-brown or black.

But you also have to take your eye color and natural hair color into consideration.

Avoid color combinations that will cause people to make unintentional associations: Pairing red and green will make people think of Christmas, black and yellow can turn you into a bumble bee, green tops and brown bottoms will make you look like a tree. Humans make some associations regardless of your intent.

7

PHOTOS & VIDEOS

They are called "professionals" for a reason.
Not everything is a good DIY idea.

How should you approach your promotional photos and your videos? I'm not going to go into the technical aspects of equipment and set-up, but just the general idea and theory of how to present yourself on film.

So, I'm assuming that you've already dialed your clothing. At this point, you want to make sure that your style—like we talked about—is consistent with your brand positioning, and it makes sense. That goes for hair, as well; what does your hairstyle look like? What does it bring to mind when people look at it? Here, again, you can get help from a professional, once you are able to articulate who you are and the brand positioning you are going for. "Here's who I want to be in the world." This will give these professionals, who are artists, an opportunity to help you craft that look.

You want to make sure that, in your photos and videos, you are projecting the same, consistent look, top to bottom. Now, that doesn't mean you can't do an occasional, *Hey, I'm at home, I'm comfortable in my sweats, and I'm just doing a quick video*—as long as you frame it correctly. You can do that, but make sure that your head-to-toe look is congruent with your brand positioning; don't get lazy.

Photos

These could be some of the most crucial assets you'll create for yourself, and it is important that you hire somebody who is great at capturing humans in photographs. Here's why.

Let's say you go out and get your cousin's friend who was recommended from a Facebook post, and that photographer usually shoots food for magazine ads. He might be able to get you to strike a pose, but he won't know how to get your authentic, real look. There's a thing that I call "good face." If you don't have good face in a photo, it's just inauthentic. It looks like a pose. It looks like a statue. It looks like you're auditioning for some kind of modeling shoot or commercial. It doesn't even seem like you're a real human.

You've got to understand that people judge you based on your face within a tenth of a second. We've already made an association with you when we first see your photos, when we first see your face. You need to make sure that face is authentic, well-lit, and professional. How does it pair with your clothes (are they congruent with the style that you've put together?) and hair (do you have some crazy piece of hair flying out to the side that makes it look unprofessional?) A pro can catch all those little things for you, so that you can just focus on being comfortable during the photo shoot. Don't you dare use your everyday photos that your friends took at a party. I'm talking about your main brand photos—the ones you'll use on a book cover, Facebook profile, or website. You really should have a set of professional photos that capture who you are and that can be used for a variety of assets.

Videos

Videos are so much fun, because they are appropriate for all kinds of content. If you're a video person, you can be creative—you can have titles and music, you can do outdoor lifestyle stuff, and all kinds of fun, different variants of videos.

But here's the thing I want you to understand: be mindful, again, of your top-line brand positioning. How do you want to be seen? What kind of reputation are you trying to create? Whom do you want to attract?

Start with adjusting your filming background. If you're setting up in your home to do some sort of content piece to share with your audience, what's behind you? It matters.

You're going to get judged and assessed by your base of viewers on all these little things, so make sure they're congruent with what you want to communicate.

Your lighting is critical in video. I don't want to see shadows across your face. Light yourself really well. Getting a ring light solves that problem out of the gate. Consider investing in a basic ring light for yourself, so you're well-lit and people can see your lovely face.

Now, how about you, and what you're going to say? Take into account your tone, your words, and your body language. What are you doing? Are you slouched down in the chair? Because that communicates even more than what's coming out of your mouth. How you're sitting, how you're standing—be very aware of what all that body language is communicating. Confidence, or lack thereof, can get in the way of your words so to mute your message.

What I would recommend you do after you record a video is to share it with someone you trust. Just get a fresh pair of eyes on it. "Hey, how does that land for you?" "Anything weird you notice in there?" Do that for awhile, until you start to cultivate the skill set of shooting videos and hitting all those points on your own.

Get a fresh pair of eyes on it.

Watch the length of your videos, as well. Sometimes we can get very excited about our own content and just talk, and talk, and talk about a thing, and people will tune out quickly. Make sure you do a chin check on yourself and say, "Wait a minute, did I ramble on too long? Did I get the point? Can I say this more concisely? How about I try this again, and be a little more to the point, or smile, or have fun with it?"

Get the message out, but show some personality, you know? Because at the end of the day, the video is not for you—it's to share with other people. Make sure that it's something other people want to watch. If you're bored by your own video when you watch it, there's a good chance everyone else will be too. The length and the energy you project throughout your video will either keep or kill the viewers' attention.

I want you to know that your first few videos are probably going to be bad, and that's okay, because there's very few people that, out of the gate, have incredible videos. Don't let that stop you. Just practice. Keep getting better. Keep assessing. Keep watching. Keep getting feedback, and improve over time. I promise you, you'll look back, and think, "Wow, I'm on video twenty, or whatever, at this point, and I look so much better! I'm more comfortable and confident."

That's part of the deal. You've got to get those videos made and out there in order to improve. You don't have to post them all, or any of them, until you're happy with what you see. Don't be afraid to get started.

SUMMARY

Photo Tips

Again, I strongly recommend a professional photo shoot for your personal brand. It's important to hire a professional photographer who specializes in shooting humans. Professionals are trained to make sure everything is perfect to capture the best you.

- *Clothing.* Dress your best with help from the experts.

- *Hairstyle.* Get help from professional stylists.

- *Background.* Make sure everything that will be captured on camera is adding to the image you're going for. Refer to your expert positioning.

Here are some pointers to help you take great photos, either at home or with a photographer. Simple poses and lighting tips will help you get those great shots.

- For front-facing headshots or (selfies), right lighting is key.

- A big wall that has light reflecting on it—as opposed to a small, exposed bulb—is ideal for selfie-taking.

- To put your best face forward, your lighting needs to be on your level.

- Along with keeping your lighting at eye level, you want to make sure you're facing in the right direction when you take selfies, to make the most of the light.

- If you have white walls or white tile, the light coming in will reflect back into your face. But, a room with dark colors will wash you out and is probably a bad choice. Strive for something in between.

Recommended Shots

Headshot

Staring straight ahead into the camera is not typically a flattering look. Instead, angle your head ever so slightly to the right or left.

Profile

Relax! Whether you use a phone or a traditional camera, your pose should be natural for you.

Three-Quarters

For the most slimming position, angle your body slightly to one side, one foot in front of the other, shoulders back, pelvis thrust out, and stomach sucked in. This might sound odd, but take it step by step and get all those elements right, and it will work out.

Full Body

Take simple head-to-toe shots in various standing positions.

Waist-Up

Don't position your head and shoulders the same way. Instead, turn your shoulders away from the camera slightly while turning your head toward it. This helps avoid a double chin and is slimming.

Remember to have fun!

Video Tips

The above elements become even more critical on video, because viewers will be watching them longer than they'll glance at a photo.

- Check yourself. Hair, clothing, shine, teeth.

- Check your background. Make sure it's on brand!

- Check your lighting. Buy a basic ring light.

- Check your tone. Posture, body language, attitude.

- Be mindful of what you're saying in your videos. Make sure everything is consistent with how you want to be seen.

- Watch your time and make sure that you are being clear and concise. Make sure it stays on track and holds attention.

- Share your video with someone you trust.

- Your first few videos aren't going to be great unless you've been trained. Keep improving, and you'll become more comfortable.

Remember: Stay consistent in your photos and videos.

Checklist: Some Quick Gear to Get You Started on Your Vlog.

This entire setup (minus the phone) will cost you less than $600. This is all you need for now.

- Any iPhone or Android made in the last 2 years

- Tripod or Table-top Tripod with phone adapter

- Shotgun Microphone

- Ring Light

- Lavalier Microphone

- Stabilizer (DJI-Osmo, for example)

8

COPY

It's okay if you aren't Shakespeare. Interesting content beats correct punctuation every time.

L et's talk copy. Copywriting is a thing that freaks a lot of people out. Oftentimes, folks get uncomfortable with the idea of writing because they think, "Oh, my grammar, or my spelling, or punctuation isn't the best," or maybe, "I don't feel like I'm smart enough when I write."

Let me assure you: that is not a problem. Get over it. Here's why. Two reasons:

First, you can always hire an editor. You can write your stuff—just your raw, stream-of-thought—and then you can send that to somebody with an outline of what you're trying to accomplish with the piece. A professional editor will make it all polished and beautiful to your specifications.

There are several freelance hiring platforms out there, which I'll list later.

Second, you can just let imperfect copy go out into the market and own it. Say, "Hey, I wasn't very smart in school, and I don't care. Here's what I have to say. I might misspell things. My grammar may not be correct, but what I have to tell you is more important than that." Get ahead of it, address it, knock it out of the way. That's fine. Because I can assure you, if your message and your content are authentic and pure and awesome, and people can feel the intent behind what you're doing, they're not going to go away because you had a typo. Trust me; that's not going to get in the way.

> *Just make sure that what you're saying,*
> *what you're sharing, is valuable and awesome—period.*
> *End of story.*

I know you can relate, because you would probably feel the same way if you were to read an article and there were typos everywhere, but what you read was so valuable that you actually could take action on it in your life. You're like, "Dude, this really made a difference for me." You wouldn't go, "It sucked, because there was a typo." Let it go. Focus on the message.

I want you to be aware of your words when you write. When we talk about tone, and voice, imagine that the reader is hearing some sort of tone or voice in their head while they're reading this to themselves. You want to make sure that this tone and voice is accurate and in line with who you want to be and how you want to be seen.

How do you speak? Make sure it's the same. If someone reads a piece from you and then they watch a video, they want to realize that it's the same person. I can tell it's your writing, because you kind of speak the same way.

RULE OF BRAND: *Always be intentional about the value you're trying to provide with your message. Stay authentic ,and don't try to be anyone but yourself. Write how you speak, and just be you.*

So, write how you speak. Be true to that.

The thing to be aware of when you're writing—and again, it depends on the use case—but in general, a good rule of thumb is, each piece is supposed to get people to want to read the next line and the next paragraph and the next section, and actually *read the entire thing,* especially when it's sales copy and you're trying to drive someone to a behavior at the end. But in either case, you want to be aware that this piece is designed to keep people's interest, to hook them and then to continue to hold their hand through the process, to the point where they can't wait to read the next piece and finishing the entire article or post, whatever it may be.

So, you have to practice. You're going to have to get good at that, because it takes time if you're not a natural writer to understand how to write persuasively and keep people interested. Just start writing, start getting it out there, and pay attention to user feedback. They're going to comment and say things. Interact with them. Respond. Adjust your writing the next time.

"Hey guys, what did you think? How did you like that piece? What could I do to get better?" People love giving their opinions, so leverage that kind of human behavior and get the feedback, so that you can grow as a writer.

It's most important that you're always authentic and express who you are and your brand. Do not try to sound like something else. That's the worst mistake you could make; to try to pretend or posture like you're something else or someone else. It's just a brand-killer; so don't do that. Always be true to you, keep it real. People like you just the way you are. That's why they're following you. They like you, so don't be afraid to be that.

SUMMARY

We're not all talented writers, but you can't let that hold you back from sharing your value. Don't let copywriting scare you.

Hire an editor to check your articles and posts. Fiverr is a cost-effective online platform that allows you to hire an outsourcer for a very reasonable price. Give it a try. It's a lot easier than you think, once you get going.

The other option, if you don't want to hire an editor, is to put it all out there anyway. As long as what you're saying provides value, not many people are going to care if there's a grammar mistake. Would you hold it against someone who provided content you loved?

Remember: Write how you speak. Just be you. Always stay authentic, and don't try to be anyone but yourself. And always provide value.

Have you ever read something that was so powerful that typos didn't matter? Sure you have. If your content is quality and your intent is pure, your audience won't turn against you.

Remember: The key is getting started.

In general, each piece you write is meant to lead to the next. So you want to leave your audience with a pleasant experience with every post, paragraph, or interaction with your written brand.

Hook them and hold their hand through the entire piece. Pretend you are writing to a ten-year-old with a very short attention span. You need to guide them where to go, or they'll lose focus. Snap your fingers if you need to! Keep them interested, and don't be afraid to push them along.

Look over what you first write, and then go back over your language. Choose words that cause the right impression. If you aren't able to objectively gauge the tone of your writing, ask someone for a second opinion. Get feedback that will help you get better. People love providing feedback.

Remember: People like you for who you are!

9

DESIGN

*Keeping design simple is the hardest lesson
for people to learn.*

This is a very tricky topic because, a lot of times, folks believe that their preference for a logo or a book cover or a photo is the thing to design around. Unless you have a well-trained eye for art and design, you can get yourself in a position where you've got a logo or colors and design experiences that are just not awesome (and I'm being nice.)

Let's go back to the example of these general agreements with humans on what is aesthetically pleasing. Again, the purple car with the gold trim, and the pink rims, and the red seats—that's just an eyesore that throws you off. We don't want that. We want the vehicle for your message and brand to be welcoming, and we want it to communicate who you are. We want it to be attractive. We want people to stay in your home and not be put off by some odd design ideas.

Let me just give you some basics that you can be aware of when you're designing things like your logo, and your website layout, or flyers, or business cards… things like that.

One is the color theory, those color principles we talked about: pairing the right colors that go together. If you need to use other people in your life whom you trust to give you a candid opinion, you can. I caution you on that, as well, because everyone has their own filter. And lots of times, people you know will just tell you that whatever you did looks great. It may be best to take the advice of a professional who's skilled in design. But if you do DIY, just be aware that color pairing is important, which things go together. Never forget that awful car example.

Think of your house. If you're pairing two colors together on your home, what do you think would be pleasing? What do you think would be attractive to folks driving by going, "Oh, that's very nice, what a beautiful home. That's a nice home." Think about that.

Be aware of the symmetry of things, especially when you start talking about logos and the balance of content and images. Humans unconsciously are repelled by things that are off, symmetrically. If you have one side of your logo a little lopsided because your cousin did it who isn't a really great designer but you're like, "Hey, I have 'Polar Bear Car

Wash' as my business," and he worked up a cool polar bear in a circle, and he's holding a sponge, but the sponge is oddly shaped, and it's bigger than his head… These are the kinds of balance considerations you need to have, and the best way to address that is to simplify. Simple, simple, simple.

RULE OF BRAND: *Keep design elements simple. When it comes to digital website design, less is always more.*

Think of the spacing. White space is awesome, because it lets people breathe. It lets people zero in on something simple—a simple design element. Maybe it's a letter, maybe it's just a signature. Think of examples like Oprah's magazine masthead. You know exactly what it is—the "O" with the little scribbly other part. It just makes sense to the brain, and it doesn't get in the way of the message.

The more complicated you get, the more cluttered you get, the more out of balance things are. This cuts people off from your message, and those are the things that can stop them from going further into your brand. Poor design is distracting.

People feel—they don't know why—"I just don't like this, " and guess what? It's part of your brand ecosystem. If they don't like one part, they often will judge the whole that way. You have to be very aware of this.

Each part represents the whole, so make sure that each part is congruent and consistent and clear.

So, let me just say a little bit more about your logo and give you best practices on how to approach your logo design.

Your logo is not supposed to be a distraction. It's not supposed to stick *out*, it's supposed to stick in the mind. It also is powerful when it's subtle. Which logos automatically pop in your mind when you hear the word *logo?* Probably McDonald's, Nike, Apple, because their simple imagery just sticks—the golden arches, the swoosh, the apple. They're simple—super simple, and they have you focus on a certain element.

What do you want your audience to focus on? When you start moving into illustrations, the more complicated an image is, the more difficult it is to stick in the mind. Some companies pull it off—Starbucks, for example—but for you, as a human brand, I want you to simplify, because it's not all about your logo. It's about the entire brand ecosystem. It's about you. It's about your message. It's about your reputation. It's about how you make people feel. You want that to pop to mind instantly.

So make it very, very simple, and don't get in your own way. Did I say "simple" enough times?

SUMMARY

You want your brand assets to be designed so they are welcoming and attractive. Sadly, most people rely on *their* preference, rather than what an audience wants to see, which often leads to disaster. But that just means you'll stand out that much more if you have professional help.

Remember: They're called professionals for a reason. Invest in a good designer, photographer, writer, or videographer.

Let me give you some basics that you can be aware of when you're designing your assets. Be aware of the symmetry of things. Look at the balance of things. People are thrown off when things are out of kilter.

Keep Design Simple

Simplify. Use basic elements and allow a lot of white space, so the audience can breathe and doesn't get overwhelmed. The more complicated you get, the more cluttered you get, the more it distracts your audience, and they may lose interest.

Logo Tips

Likewise, your logo shouldn't be a distraction. It should be simple and powerful. Your brand is about you and how you make people feel. You don't want to blow that up by choosing a crazy logo. Remember, a logo is just another asset—another extension of you and your brand.

Keep your focus on one element in your logo, such as the curve in the McDonald's golden arches, or Oprah's "O."

Be deliberate. What do you want the viewer to focus on and why? Stick to one element to concentrate on.

Remember: Don't complicate or overthink it.

10

OUTSOURCING

*Managers and leaders know the importance
of delegation. There's nothing wrong with making
your life easier and more efficient while you focus
on the bigger picture.*

Outsourcing has been the bane of my existence. We all
need help at some point; but it's hard to get good help!

Seriously. I have outsourced for years, and I've tried it
all. In this section, I'm going to help you avoid the pain
and suffering that I've experienced with this puzzle piece.
Because it's critical, it's important to outsource at times; but,
done wrong, can definitely be "not fun."

Face it: there are things you're just not great at. You did
the strengths and weaknesses analysis of yourself earlier. So
you've got to know where you're weak and which things
are dragging you down. This awareness will tell you when

it's time to outsource. You sitting there spending a month building your own website is probably not the best use of your time. Or your logo, or whatever components you know you're not great at. Outsource them! There are really cost-effective ways to do it.

So, the first thing you have to do is understand how to outsource. How does it work? There are tons of platforms you can go to, but first, you have to know how to interact with contractors and freelancers. You've got to know what you're going into, so that you can manage your own expectations and be prepared.

The first thing you want to do is get clear on the objective. What do you want from these folks you're about to outsource to? Are you clear on the asset that you want or the outcome that you want? If you're not clear, this is where the mess starts to occur, especially if you work with contractors from other countries. Then you might have a language barrier and an interpretation barrier to deal with as well. That's a big challenge. To get the best result for your money, what I've learned is that you have to be very, very clear in your communication early on when you're talking to outsourcers.

Tell them, "Here's exactly what I expect," and then ask clarifying questions to make sure they understand the task.

Additionally, you need to ask to look at their portfolio. You need to see that they've done the thing that you're about to hire them to do. No email chain and testimonials can replace actually seeing the end result of the experience.

RULE OF BRAND: *If you're outsourcing a logo or design, look at their portfolio to see they've provided the quality of work you want.*

Look at the logos they've done. That way, you have a sense of their style and their aesthetic. What you're looking for is the person or the team that has executed really well, to your standards, in the past. And you find that in their portfolio.

The other thing I believe is that relationships end how they begin. So, if you're communicating with an outsource agency or person, and the communication is awful, and it's hard to get them to understand things, and you're struggling to hear back from them—that's exactly how your project is going to go. My suggestion is to cut bait and run. Find someone else.

It always ends how it starts. So, you're looking for someone who, from the very beginning, understands what you want and can communicate clearly what they will do to get you there.

There are a number of resources and places you can go to find great people, like Fiverr, 99Designs, Upwork … these are all places to outsource design work.

Make sure you understand what a "scope of work" should look like. After you fill out the creative brief for these folks—your description of what you want—they're going to send you back a scope of work. It should outline, "Hey, here's our understanding in general. Here's what we're going to do for you, and when it will be done." You need to know what to expect, so you can hold them accountable and help them produce what you envision.

SUMMARY

Revisit your strengths and weaknesses, and identify which things are dragging you down. These are the tasks you are going to want to pass off to an outsourcer. But first you must understand how to outsource and manage expectations.

Outsourcing Tips

1. Be clear on your objective. What *exactly* do you want from the outsourcer? This saves time and money.

2. Beware of language and interpretation barriers.

3. Ask clarifying questions. Make them repeat all instructions back to you.

4. Look at their portfolio!

5. Look for a team who has executed to your standards.

6. Make sure communication works in the beginning. Or run.

Remember: Relationships end how they begin.

Outsourcing Checklist and Resources

Here are a few questions you might want to ask while vetting the team that handles your brand.

- Have you built successful brands for entrepreneurs in a similar position to where I am at currently?

- What have your previous clients experienced as a result of your branding efforts?

- What is your process for building brands specifically for individuals and entrepreneurs?

- How do you decide what color scheme to use for individuals?

- How many people will be working on my brand at any given time?

- Who is on your team and how are they an expert in their respective discipline?

When looking at their portfolio, ask yourself these questions.

- Has this team produced the types of content you want to provide?

- Is their work flawless in design and logic?

- Do they create easy-to-use user experiences for their clients' audiences?

- Is their work compelling and engaging?

- Does it pull the reader in and demand attention?

Popular Outsource Resources For Design, Copy & Other Creative Service

Fiverr

99designs

Upwork

Writer's Access

Book Butchers

A creative brief that you'll provide explains the details of the project for the creative team or designer. You'll want to be as granular and specific as possible in order to get back the high quality you're looking for.

A scope of work is then delivered to you and outlines the job the team is doing for you, so you know what to expect.

This is why having clarity on all the things you've learned so far *before* creating your brand assets or outsourcing is critical. Knowing who you are, what you want, your story, your expert positioning, who you want to attract, your values, and other human brands you like will help you inform the professionals you hire, so you can get the right assets created.

This is where most people fail. They start hiring people to build things for them, just hoping they'll like what they produce. Then they wonder why the assets are all over the place, don't represent who they are, and need to be redone numerous times. Contractors are not mind readers. But tell them what you want, specifically, and the good ones will deliver.

I know this doesn't apply to you, because you're putting in the work you've learned here and will do it right. Right?

Go on with your bad self!

THE WRAP-UP

Your perfect fans, partners, employees, and customers would love to meet, follow, and buy from you right now ... they just have no idea you exist.

Ask yourself these questions constantly while working on your brand:

- What do I want people to know about me?

- How do I want them to feel when they see my website or social channels?

- How do I want them to feel when they see my image or hear me speak?

- What experience do I want to leave them with?

- What value do I plan to give to the world without asking a damn thing in return?

- What do I want to cause in the world?

- What reputation do I want to be known for?

Use the answers to these questions, along with your story, big dreams, big ideas, values, and your "why," as the nucleus of your brand. This is your North Star.

You deserve to be heard, and the world deserves your gifts. The world needs to hear from you now, more than ever. ***Stop being invisible and build a brand of greater influence.***

You know, I've built businesses. I've made and lost millions. I've lived out some of my greatest childhood dreams. I'm now in a phase of life where I want to spend more time with my wife and kids, while still being a serial entrepreneur and launching new and exciting things.

I built Bad People because I wanted to build my last business. A business that would allow me to experience the flavors of new ideas, businesses, and projects without actually having to be the CEO every time. An umbrella brand that could house a team of creativity. I wanted to create a legacy for my family as being the guy who helped shape the world by lifting up countless heroes. I wanted one business that could serve others and fulfill my need for variety, visual beauty, storytelling, and ideation of new products. So, I created it.

Human branding allows me to do all of this. I have so many ideas and change that I want to bring to the world that it would be impossible to do all of them on my own. I had an "aha!" moment when I realized that the best way for me to impact the world on a massive scale was to help as many talented humans realize their individual missions for change.

It's like helping create an army of superheroes. It's my way of giving back. I'm good at it. And I love it.

Thank you for trusting me enough to listen to my story and hear my advice. I hope this book can help you realize and communicate your superpowers to the world.

I would be so grateful to hear from you. What did you think about this book? What did you like or dislike about it? Please don't hesitate to reach out on social media and let me know. I can currently be reached @MeetDion on Instagram and LinkedIn or my website at www.dionmcintosh.com.

–Dion McIntosh

ABOUT THE AUTHOR

I was born in the seventies and bounced around from neighborhood to neighborhood. All different types. But I stayed focused and kept my act clean … for the most part. I'm a native of Seattle's inner city and the son of a powerhouse single mom, who taught me that opportunity doesn't knock—you have to go get her attention. She taught me to always be bold and humble, be excellent at everything you do, do what you say, treat people right, and be grateful along the way.

From an early age, I had this crazy ability to blend and make others see me as I wanted to be seen. Perception became a sort of game to me, and I was always building new characters to level up. This probably had something to do with my childhood obsession with video games. My first love, even more than games, was music.

I knew I was destined for a bigger pond.

I started competing in talent shows, performing on stage, and joining musicals at age seven. By fifteen, I was hustling homemade demo tapes for my R&B group. At sixteen, I got signed to Hollywood Records. So, while most kids were figuring out their awkward stage and learning how to interact with their classmates, I was learning how to craft my brand to appeal to a much larger audience—the entire world.

As the lead singer/songwriter of a marginally successful, major-label boy band, I toured the world throughout the nineties, immersed in every aspect of the music business. But I was completely captivated by the power of branding and marketing. I loved visual design and message crafting.

Well, nothing lasts forever. After a political/financial/legal fiasco, my label crumbled, and I found myself looking for a new path. If I'm no longer a singer ... what am I?

I caught the entrepreneur bug in my twenties and started failing forward, trying different things, looking to replace that feeling from the boy band glory days. I wandered the planet searching for my "thing." I started my own computer repair business, a web design company, door-to-door sales and network marketing businesses. I even had a six-month run in a J.O.B. Eventually, I left my hometown of Seattle and landed in real estate development in Los Angeles, where I met my goddess and wife, Amy.

Real estate is where I had my first huge win. And loss. Washington Mutual went bankrupt, and my business went down with them.

I was forced to walk away from millions in assets.
There I was, back at ground zero. My wife, Amy was
pregnant, and we had a one-year-old at home.
... and I was tapped the fuck out.

This was a depressing time in my life. I spent a few years rebuilding and sorting through the rubble to find my teeth. I used my failure to fuel success—moving on to architect and run dozens of companies in corporate and small business consulting, creative services, video production, digital marketing, and SAAS tech.

It's not as if it was easy. But once I started really understanding what was truly motivating and driving me, I was unstoppable. Understanding myself and what made me tick (or not tick) was the key. I finally figured out what I was searching for. After another nearly catastrophic business blow that left me $99 billion in the hole (I'll save that story for another time) I pivoted and landed on my feet—only this time, I was crystal clear on the mission. It was time to go all in and create my pièce de résistance.

I had only four requirements:

1. It had to be with the right humans.

2. I had to deeply give a shit about the thing I was building.

3. It had to make life better for the planet and/or its inhabitants.

4. It had to be scalable enough to take care of my team and our families (Top Ramen days are over.).

So, Bad People was born.

At forty-five years young, I started my ninth major venture and passion project, Bad People. I am the proud leader of a bunch of misfit ninjas who amplify the big ideas and personal brands of bad-ass entrepreneurs into great things in the world.

Life is amazing. My kids are happy, healthy, and crazy. Marriage is beautiful, passionate, and perfectly dysfunctional. I'm no longer wandering the planet in search of my "thing." I am living my passion every single day, hustling hard to help people realize their big dreams. I can't go wrong with my incredible superwoman wife by my side and my team of Bad People.

ABOUT BAD PEOPLE

Bad People is a collaboration of expert artisans coming together to push the world to progress through the positive agendas of the individuals we serve. We believe that every bad-ass company, project, or social movement starts with bad-ass humans or, as we call them, Bad People. Those who have what it takes to make things better for the planet and its inhabitants.

We help these Bad People uncover their true selves and get their messages heard, amplifying their brand above the market noise.

Their life's work is our artwork.

Want Our Professional Help?

Let's Connect:
www.BadPeople.LA

SPECIAL PROJECTS

While you're here I'd love to share some of my passion projects with you.

DEAR AMY

I'm so proud of what my wife Amy "Frankie Jordan" McIntosh has created. Over the last 4 years she has built the world's most accurate and successful Amy Winehouse Tribute show, Dear Amy. You have to see this for yourself!

Check It Out:
@dearamyband on IG
www.DearAmyBand.com

DO IT
YOURSELF
BRANDING

Created by the founding team at Bad People.la, this passion project was built to provide resources to those who don't have big budgets for the fancy pants full service branding.

Check It Out:
www.DoItYourselfBranding.com

www.ingramcontent.com/pod-product-compliance
Lightning Source LLC
Chambersburg PA
CBHW071349090426
42738CB00012B/3068